# Metal Detecting Made Easy:

## A Guide for Beginners and Reference for All

**David Villanueva**

**Published by True Treasure Books**

www.truetreasurebooks.net

**ISBN 9780955032578**

# Contents

# 1. Introduction

Metal detecting is a very rewarding hobby. Just swinging a detector on a warm sunny day in pleasant surroundings is a real pleasure in itself. Not only is there the prospect of making a major find in amongst the interesting coins and artefacts you will uncover but the hobby's many benefits include anticipation of the unknown, collecting, education, exercise, excitement, family involvement, fun, new friends. And history – like it was never taught in school!

Over thousands of years, literally many millions of coins and metal artefacts have been lost, mislaid or buried on land and beaches and in rivers and the sea. Armed with a metal detector you can bring history to life. Perhaps you will discover a roman brooch in your back yard or a Piece of Eight, on a beach, from a Spanish wreck or over a thousand Saxon gold and silver artefacts in a farmer's field, like Terry Herbert, who found the famous UK Staffordshire Hoard. Even a humble find can lead to an exciting quest of discovery as to what it is, what it was used for, who owned it and why you found it where you did.

Metal detecting is one of the greatest hobbies suitable for either sex of any age from three to 103+, with the very real possibility that at any moment you can change history, or even your life, forever.

However, unless you are extremely lucky, you are unlikely to beg, borrow or buy a metal detector and start making great finds with it from day one – you need to know a few things first. That is the purpose of this manual – to show you what equipment you need, how and where to use it and how to overcome any obstacles along the way. And much, much more...You will become a successful metal detectorist in no time.

Good Hunting!


**NB:** To avoid the following text reading like a conventional address book, I have frequently referred to outside resources by an Internet website address (URL) only. I appreciate that not everyone has Internet access, so if that is you and you are not able to gain information you require, please visit your local public library, with this book for reference and they will be happy to help you get what you need in a form that suits you.

## 2. The Basics – What You Need to Know

Every sport or recreational activity has its rules and metal detecting is no exception, so lets get that out of the way and then we can get on with the fun stuff.

Firstly, there are a number of laws affecting ownership of what we find and these are covered in the section on Treasure Law. Secondly, all land is owned by someone so you can't just go metal detecting anywhere you like – you need to obtain permission from the landowner. However, any land you own and public beaches are generally OK to metal detect on providing there are no legal restraints.

While searching beaches and tidal rivers is not everyone's idea of fun they are places where you can generally metal detect either without the formality of obtaining permission or, in some cases, you can buy a permit to search. While, there are many beaches and tidal river foreshores in private ownership, the usual 'ownership' in Britain is local Council above high water mark and Crown below.

The Crown now has a free annual permit system in place which will effectively cover all foreshore in England, Northern Ireland, Scotland and Wales under their control. The foreshore is defined as: the area between mean high and mean low water (spring tides in Scotland). A foreshore permit can be simply applied for on line at their website: http://www.thecrownestate.co.uk/metal-detecting Maps showing Crown foreshore in many areas can also be downloaded from the website.

Alternatively to obtain a permit for foreshores in England, Northern Ireland or Wales send a letter or email (enquiries@thecrownestate.co.uk) to:

The Crown Estate
Marine Department
16 New Burlington Place
London
W1S 2HX

In Scotland, everyone has a statutory right of access to beaches, foreshores and the countryside in general for outdoor pursuits, apparently including responsible metal detecting, so no permit is necessary. There are obviously a number of restrictions such as cultural heritage and archaeological sites so check out the Scottish Outdoor Access Code: http://www.outdooraccess-scotland.com/outdoors-responsibly/your-access-rights/

In the case of the river Thames, the Port of London Authority effectively owns the foreshore and runs a three-year permit system, backdated to the preceding 1st of January (unless applied for or renewed between December and January), for metal detecting between Teddington and the Thames Barrier. The current fee is £55.00 (day permit: £20). See the National Council for Metal Detecting Website: http://www.ncmd.co.uk/ for conditions and an application form. Applications to:

Mr K Jackelman
Port of London of Authority
London River House
Royal Pier Road
Gravesend
Kent DA12 2BG

Tel: 01474 562339

Email: foreshorepermits@pla.co.uk

Public beaches are usually accessible for metal detecting. There may be local bylaws however, which must be adhered to for the sake of the hobby. Bylaws will usually restrict detecting to early mornings and evenings during the holiday season. This is for the benefit of all beach users and, whether bylaws exist or not, you shouldn't be searching with a metal detector around sunbathers and others enjoying the beach, unless you have been asked specifically to find some newly lost property. It is just bad manners as well as being a very inefficient way to search.

Private beaches where the public has free access are usually equally accessible for metal detecting as the public variety, (although strictly you should seek permission from the owner). In many cases you won't be able to tell the difference. However, do look out for notices, which may affect access or searching. Private, Keep Out, means just that, unless you obtain permission and bear in mind the restriction may be because of danger. Ministry of Defence (MOD) property is a case in point. Some beaches and foreshores are designated Sites of Special Scientific Interest (SSSI) and while pedestrian access may be allowed, metal detecting is prohibited. The National Trust (or regional equivalents) owns quite a number of beaches and will not usually allow metal detecting without a good reason. However, they will seldom own the entire beach and foreshore so it is quite possible to work around their area of ownership, provided you find out from e.g. Ordnance Survey maps what area they own. Some hotels own beaches for the enjoyment of their guests. You may be able to gain permission out-of-season and you could offer to search for guests' lost property in-season.

The situation with non-tidal waterways or watercourses is somewhat different. A landowner with a frontage along a watercourse is presumed to own the bed up to the centre of the watercourse. Obviously if the same landowner owns both banks then he owns the entire bed. Unless there is proof to the contrary.

6

Sometimes errors in land deals occur and the bed is not transferred with the land, sometimes beds are bought and sold separately. The usual case with working canals and some rivers is that ownership is vested in the navigation authority by Act of Parliament to facilitate control over the use of the waterway.

While detecting non-tidal watercourses does require permission from the landowner, notwithstanding the rights of other users such as anglers, permission may be easier to obtain than that on the surrounding land. Not only that, like beaches and foreshores, watercourses are potentially a year round site and benefit from replenishment.

The code of practice in the following section is basically voluntary but there are some legal requirements and much common sense included so it would be a good idea to follow the code as closely as you can even if you live outside of England and Wales.

## 2.1. Code of Practice for Responsible Detecting in England and Wales

### Being responsible means:

#### Before you go metal-detecting

1. Not trespassing; before you start detecting obtain permission to search from the landowner/occupier, regardless of the status, or perceived status, of the land. Remember that all land has an owner. To avoid subsequent disputes it is always advisable to get permission and agreement in writing first regarding the ownership of any finds subsequently discovered (see http://www.cla.org.uk / http://www.nfuonline.com).

2. Adhering to the laws concerning protected sites (e.g. those defined as Scheduled Monuments or Sites of Special Scientific Interest: you can obtain details of these from the landowner/occupier, Finds Liaison Officer, Historic Environment Record or at http://www.magic.gov.uk). Take extra care when detecting near protected sites: for example, it is not always clear where the boundaries lie on the ground.

3. You are strongly recommended to join a metal detecting club or association that encourages co-operation and responsive exchanges with other responsible heritage groups. Details of metal detecting organizations can be found at http://www.ncmd.co.uk / http://www.fid.newbury.net.

4. Familiarising yourself with and following current conservation advice on the handling, care and storage of archaeological objects (see http://www.finds.org.uk).

#### While you are metal-detecting

5. Wherever possible working on ground that has already been disturbed (such as ploughed land or that which has formerly been ploughed), and only within the depth of ploughing. If detecting takes place on undisturbed pasture, be careful to ensure that no damage is done to the archaeological value of the land, including earthworks.

6. Minimising any ground disturbance through the use of suitable tools and by reinstating any excavated material as neatly as possible. Endeavour not to damage stratified archaeological deposits.

7. Recording findspots as accurately as possible for all finds (i.e. to at least a one hundred metre square, using an Ordnance Survey map or hand-held Global Positioning Systems (GPS) device) whilst in the field. Bag finds individually and record the National Grid Reference (NGR) on the bag. Findspot information should not be passed on to other parties without the agreement of the landowner/occupier (see also clause 9).

8. Respecting the Country Code (leave gates and property as you find them and do not damage crops, frighten animals, or disturb ground nesting birds, and dispose properly of litter: see http://www.countrysideaccess.gov.uk).

After you have been metal-detecting

9. Reporting any finds to the relevant landowner/occupier; and (with the agreement of the landowner/occupier) to the Portable Antiquities Scheme, so the information can pass into the local Historic Environment Record. Both the Country Land and Business Association (http://www.cla.org.uk) and the National Farmers Union (http://www.nfuonline.com) support the reporting of finds. Details of your local Finds liaison Officer can be found at http://www.finds.org.uk, email info@finds.org.uk or phone 020 7323 8611.

10. Abiding by the provisions of the Treasure Act and Treasure Act Code of Practice (http://www.finds.org.uk), wreck law (http://www.mcga.gov.uk) and export licensing (http://www.mta.gov.uk). If you need advice your local Finds Liaison Officer will be able to help you.

11. Seeking expert help if you discover something large below the ploughsoil, or a concentration of finds or unusual material, or wreck remains, and ensuring that the landowner/occupier's permission is obtained to do so. Your local Finds Liaison Officer may be able to help or will be able to advise of an appropriate person. Reporting the find does not change your rights of discovery, but will result in far more archaeological evidence being discovered.

12. Calling the Police, and notifying the landowner/occupier, if you find any traces of human remains.

13. Calling the Police or HM Coastguard, and notifying the landowner/occupier, if you find anything that may be a live explosive: do not use a metal-detector or mobile phone nearby as this might trigger an explosion. Do not attempt to move or interfere with any such explosives.

## 2.2. Treasure Law

Regrettably there is no international law on metal detecting finds and the laws differ from country to country and even from State to State in the USA. Given below are a number of simplified legal definitions that could apply to metal detecting finds, together with the popular court ruling on finds made under each category. However, before you spend a lot of time and money on the hunt, you would be wise to ascertain local law on finds. It would also be prudent to have an agreement, preferably in writing, with the landowner or site owner, on the distribution of finds. It is usual to split finds, awards and rewards 50/50 between finder and landowner.

**Lost property**, which has been involuntarily parted from its owner, belongs to the owner or their heirs and if they cannot be traced, title goes to the finder. You are legally obliged to take reasonable steps to return lost property to its owner. You are unlikely to find an owner for items like modern coins, however if you find something potentially traceable such as jewelery, you should either report it to the local police or take suitable action to find the owner such as advertising in a local newspaper. In Britain, the police disclaim lost property (except cellphones) after one month.

**Mislaid property**, where the owner puts the object down and forgets about it, reverts to the site owner, if not claimed by the owner.

**Abandoned property**, which is simply thrown away, goes to the finder.

**Embedded property** refers to buried artefacts or even natural minerals, which fall outside the definition of treasure trove. Court rulings for such finds will generally be the same as for treasure trove.

**Archaeological objects or portable antiquities** may cover excavated objects as recent as 50 years old in some countries and states, which have to be reported to museum authorities or similar. A reward is often paid but check local laws. Export licences may be required (e.g. European Economic Community) before such objects can be removed from the country.

**Treasure trove**, defined as objects made substantially of gold, silver and their alloys (plus paper money) hidden or concealed for several decades, with the intention of recovery, where the owners or heirs cannot be traced. Treasure trove finds on private land normally go to the finder, providing the finder wasn't trespassing but in the UK, Treasure is normally shared equally between landowner and finder. If the finder was trespassing then finds go to the landowner or site owner. Finds on government land go to the government unless there is a prior agreement in place.

**Wreck**, being an abandoned vessel, or something abandoned off a vessel, which is afloat, stranded, aground or sunken. The salvor is normally entitled to a reward related to the value of the find

## 2.3. The Treasure Act in England and Wales

At present, treasure is defined, under the Act, as any object other than a coin, at least 300 years old when found, which has a metallic content, of which at least 10% by weight is gold or silver. And all coins that contain at least 10% by weight of gold or silver that come from the same find consisting of at least two coins, at least 300 years old. And all coins that contain less than 10% by weight gold or silver that come from the same find consisting of at least ten coins at least 300 years old. And any associated objects (e.g. a pot or other container), except unworked natural objects, found in the same place as treasure objects. And any objects or coin hoards less than 300 years old, made substantially of gold and silver that have been deliberately hidden with the intention of recovery and for which the owner is unknown. From 1 January 2003 the definition of treasure has been extended on prehistoric (i.e. up to the end of the Iron Age) finds to include all multiple artefacts, made of any metal, found together and single artefacts deliberately containing any quantity of precious metal.

The Act applies to objects found anywhere in England, Wales and Northern Ireland, including in or on land, in buildings (whether occupied or ruined), in rivers and lakes and on the foreshore (the area between mean high water and mean low water) providing the object does not come from a wreck. If the object has come from a wreck then it will be subject to the salvage regime that applies to wreck under the Merchant Shipping Act 1995. The Receiver of Wreck (located in the Maritime and Coastguard Agency, Southampton, UK) must legally be notified of all property recovered following the loss of a vessel; and the salvor is entitled to a reward related to the value of the object, either from the owner, if identified, or the Crown.

If you are searching in other parts of the British Isles or outside of Britain altogether, you should familiarize yourself with treasure law for your specific area. In Scotland, for instance, all ownerless objects belong to the Crown. They must be reported regardless of where they were found or of what they are made. The finder receives market value as long as no laws have been broken. Not all finds will be claimed. Further information from: Treasure Trove Unit, National Museum of Scotland, Chambers Street, Edinburgh, EH1 1JF.

I have the experience of having had to report eleven separate finds of treasure since the introduction of the Treasure Act. There is little wrong with the Treasure Act itself but problems can arise when the Code of Practice isn't followed. My major concern initially was the lack of confidentiality promised regarding the find spot, for it seems that a number of Coroners, in the early days, gave away fairly precise details of find spots to the Press. For the benefit of novices the implication is that if thieves, usually called 'Nighthawks', learn the location of your site they may raid it in the hope of finding more treasure

12

and may cause serious damage to the landowner's crops or other property in the process. You wouldn't blame the landowner if he then banned you from his land with his neighbors probably following suit. Painting the blackest picture, you could lose access to vast tracts of land and countless other treasures.

You are probably thinking if that is what could happen when you comply with the law you'll keep quiet when you find treasure. Unfortunately the penalty for not reporting is far greater, for if you get caught; you may be fined up to £5000 and be imprisoned for three months. You are then branded a criminal, which could seriously ruin your life.

But nowadays there are very few problems with the Treasure Act and mostly good things come from your honesty, like access to the next site and your next treasure find. Potential problems can be avoided if you know how. And you will know how by the time you've finished reading this chapter.

My first treasure find, in February 1999, was a gilt silver medieval ring brooch, unfortunately missing its sword-shaped pin, inscribed with the letters IESVSX (Jesus Christ) found, in close proximity to two contemporary silver coins. The find spot, on the site of a medieval Hundred Court, was near the boundary between two Coroners' provinces. It took three weeks to get one of them to accept responsibility as the Coroner's Officers were out most of the time and didn't return calls.

I was asked to deposit the find with a choice of three or four fairly local museums. I chose the most convenient to me and I am pleased to say the curator was very helpful. The landowner was on holiday at the time of the find and I arranged to delay depositing the items with the museum until the landowner had the opportunity to view them. When I deposited the objects in April, the curator advised putting a four-figure Ordnance Survey map reference on the Treasure Receipt and recorded the eight-figure reference separately.

The Museum didn't want to acquire the finds and after reference was made to the landowner, they were disclaimed and returned to me without fuss or publicity on 17 September 1999.

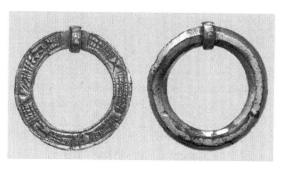

**Medieval ring brooch**

The second find began in April 1999, with the finding of a single Ambiani type E Iron Age gold stater by the landowner. This coin didn't qualify as treasure by itself and wasn't reported. On September 30, 1999, I found two more Ambiani gold staters in the same place and reported all three to the Coroner about 12 days later. (I knew who the Coroner was this time.) Because of the difficulties of my getting to a museum (at my own expense), we arranged for the finds to be deposited by the landowner at a different museum to the previous find. Based on advice previously received, I briefed the landowner on what information to put on the Treasure Receipt. With the agreement of the landowner, the curator filled in both the Treasure Receipt and the museum's standard receipt, recording eight-figure find spots together with the name of the farm on both receipts. The landowner was given the museum receipt and we were both later sent copies of the official Treasure Receipt.

During December 1999 and early January 2000, I recovered four more Ambiani staters, one by one from the same place. I reported each one to the Coroner within 14 days of each find and the four were handed over to the Museum on 10 January 2000 by the landowner. The dual receipting procedure was repeated although in answer to the landowner's comments about terms on the museum receipt, which couldn't be applied to potential treasure finds, the curator crossed out the disagreeable parts.

The inquest was originally scheduled for late January but was postponed to 24 February as a result of the additional finds. The inquest was a quiet affair with only the landowner, Coroner, two officers and myself in attendance. The coins were inevitably declared 'Treasure', the museum having an interest in acquiring them. Expenses were offered for attending court.

The Coroner's officer phoned the following day to tell me that the local Press wanted to speak to me, he also told me that he was legally obliged to reveal details of the find to the Press. I had discussions with the landowner who wanted no publicity. We decided that it would be better to speak to the Press and appeal to them not to reveal sensitive information, rather than risk them

14

making their own stories up from what they got from the Coroner's office. While one reporter made it clear that he knew the landowner's name and the name of the farm, he did act responsibly and complied with our wishes to publish neither.

The Curator took the coins to the British Museum. We (landowner and myself) then received a letter from the Department of Culture Media and Sport (who administered the Treasure Act at that time) saying the coins were being valued, the valuation would be sent to us and we would have 28 days to comment and offer alternative valuations. I did actually attempt to obtain a couple of valuations but could only get ballpark figures without the valuers being able to view the actual coins. One dealer requested £50 for this service but subsequently gave me a free retail valuation for which I was grateful.

On 11 May I received a letter from the Department of Culture Media and Sport with a valuation report from Sotheby's (£1260-£1400). The letter said that the valuation committee was sitting the following day and we were not going to be allowed to make representations on the provisional valuation owing to Public holidays.

On 16 May the Department of Culture Media and Sport advised that the committee had valued the coins at £1350 and we had one month to make representation if dissatisfied. The Museum was also allowed to make representation on the valuation. The Museum then had up to four months to settle, from the time this figure was accepted by all parties. We agreed to accept the valuation, which was close to the ballpark figures given by the dealers.

Discussing this case with Bob Whalley, Co-ordinator for Policy, National Council for Metal Detecting, it came to light that the first coin found by the landowner should not have been declared Treasure as it was only a single find at the time. The Department of Culture Media and Sport agreed. The museum wanted all seven coins to maintain the integrity of the supposed cache, however by request the coin was returned to the landowner and an agreed pro rata award, split equally between the landowner and myself, was made for the other six coins during October 2000.

After the autumn ploughing the landowner and myself found a further Ambiani stater each on the same field. I reported these to the Coroner within the stipulated 14 days and suggested we delayed handing the coins over until I had carried out further searching. As it happened, I didn't find any more, so the landowner took the two coins to the museum in mid-January 2001. The museum wanted these coins to add to the other six so they inevitably were going to be declared treasure. I was quite puzzled why the museum even wanted the coins in the first place, as Ambiani staters must be the most common Iron Age gold coins. In answer to that question the curator told me that they needed to keep them together for posterity and future research when improved analytical techniques may be able to provide more information.

Between January and the Inquest in May, the Coroner and his two officers all retired leaving a Deputy Coroner and a new officer to take charge of the case. As the Coroner's officer suggested the inquest was going to be just a brief formality, neither the landowner nor myself attended. The following day the Coroner's officer rang the landowner saying that the coins had been declared treasure and the Press had been given details, including the Landowner's telephone number. The Landowner was not happy, I was not happy and the following week when a report on the find appeared in the local paper, giving the full name and address of the farm, in the midst of the Foot and Mouth crisis, we were livid. Locally there was not much that could be done other than to ask neighbors to look out for intruders, while Bob Whalley and I moved into written complaint mode. Bob wrote to the Deputy Coroner while I tackled Doctor Roger Bland, Adviser on Treasure. We eventually received replies from Doctor Bland, the Deputy Coroner and from two other Coroners who had each inherited part of the retired Coroner's area owing to a County reorganization. The deputy Coroner said it wasn't anything to do with her any longer and couldn't comment, while one of the 'new' Coroners said she only referred to find spots by map reference. The second 'new' Coroner, on the other hand, while suggesting that information was given to the Press during the inquest, somewhat more encouragingly confirmed that her officers should not report find spots to the Press and promised to check out other possible sources of 'leaks', such as the Police Press Office.

Meanwhile the valuation was set at £440 for the two coins that the Deputy Coroner had determined had both been found by me and my attempts to rectify that verdict have fallen on deaf ears. The landowner and myself accepted the award, which was paid in January 2002, split 75% in favor of the landowner (I couldn't really claim half the value of a coin I didn't find).

16

**Gold Staters**

In June 2002 on a club search in the grounds of a medieval manor house I found, within ten minutes, a fifteenth century iconographic gold finger ring engraved with figures of Saint Catherine, a bearded male believed to be Saint John the Baptist and floral motifs. This clearly had to be reported to the Coroner. Aware of the recent reorganization in the County, I wrote to the most likely candidate from the Treasure Act Code of Practice book and asked that my letter be passed to the appropriate Coroner if that office no longer dealt with the parish where I had found the ring. My letter was passed on to another Coroner who turned out to be the lady who only refers to the find spot by map reference.

I was asked to take the ring to the museum, which had dealt with the Staters and we went straight for the Treasure Receipt this time. I only gave a four-figure map reference for the find spot to be entered on the Treasure Receipt even though the Curator wanted six. I explained why I didn't want the full find spot reference recorded on the receipt and offered it to be kept separately although that was declined for the moment. The local museum wanted the ring so it went to Treasure Inquest, which unfortunately was scheduled while I was away on holiday and I was unable to attend. There was only the briefest mention of the ring in the local newspaper, giving only the name of the parish as the find spot and I eventually received a half share in the £3750 award.

**Medieval ring**

A year (almost to the day) after finding the medieval ring, I found a Roman silver ring with a gold stud supposedly representing the evil eye to protect the wearer. I reported to the Coroner and deposited it, in exchange for a Treasure Receipt, at a different museum, which was more convenient at the time. The ring was disclaimed and returned to me with the landowner's agreement.

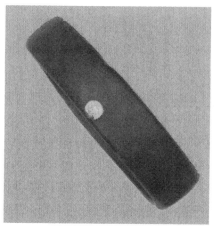

**Roman ring**

My next treasure find made, as an invited guest, on a field was a sixth century gold Saxon pendant, which I reported to the same lady Coroner as the previous two finds. By this time the County Finds Liaison Officer (FLO) had taken over the role of 'treasure receiver' as a natural extension of their administration of the Portable Antiquities Scheme, where found objects are voluntary reported for inclusion on a national finds database. I handed over the pendant to the FLO in exchange for a Treasure Receipt. The local museum wished to acquire the find so it went to inquest, which I was able to attend, where the Coroner cautioned me not to give out the find spot in court! The press were present and interviewed me after the short hearing, later publishing a small article, only revealing the name of the parish, and the photograph of the pendant, which I had given them. The division of the award here was a little tricky as legally only the finder and landowner share the award but here I was a guest and it was unfair for my friend, Shaun, who had invited me, to lose out. Shaun also felt that the tenant farmer should be rewarded. I resolved then to split my award equally between Shaun, the farmer and myself but I thought it best to tell the landowner what I was doing in case he was thinking of doing something similar. As soon as I mentioned it, the landowner said it would be best if I just shared my half with Shaun and the landowner would share his half with the farmer so the four of us ended up with equal shares in the £1300 award.

**Saxon pendant**

My seventh treasure find was a seventeenth century gold Memento Mori or mourning ring, unfortunately badly damaged by agricultural machinery. I reported this to the same Coroner as previously and handed it over to the FLO in exchange for a Treasure Receipt. Not surprisingly it was disclaimed.

**Mourning ring**

My eighth find, another small cache of Iron Age gold Staters and second addenda to the cache from the same field as previously, was declared treasure, without issues.

My ninth find was a Bronze Age founder's cache of broken axes and ingots, on which the landowner and I agreed to waive our awards so the find could be effectively donated to our local museum.

**Part of a Bronze Age founder's hoard**

My tenth and eleventh find were a single Iron Age gold stater addendum followed by two gold stater addenda to the main find, both working their way through the system at the time of writing.

Clearly there has been a vast improvement in the handling of potential treasure in my area over the past few years, however I still urge you to be cautious when reporting your finds. Here are my unofficial suggestions for protecting yourself and your landowner friends when you find potential treasure:

* Leave your treasure 'as found' and resist all temptation to clean or restore your find except for the absolute minimum necessary to identify it as possible treasure.

* The National Council for Metal Detecting will willingly advise in the process of reporting treasure and it is well worth involving them from the start when you have potential treasure to report.

* County Finds Liaison Officers (FLOs) are now heavily involved in the treasure process and will also advise and help.

* Your only legal obligation is to report the finding of potential treasure to the Coroner within fourteen days of becoming aware that it is possibly treasure. It has now become expedient for potential treasure to be reported in the first instance to the FLO, who then informs the Coroner. While I am not aware of any issues with this practice, to comply strictly with the letter of the law, I always report to the Coroner in the first instance and copy my letter to the FLO.

* Discuss the matter with the landowner as soon as possible.

* Do the reporting yourself. The legal responsibility for reporting rests with the finder and no one will look after your interests as well as you.

* Bear in mind, especially if you want to keep the coin, that the first coin found of a scattered hoard may not be treasure, if it was the only coin found on that occasion and there was sufficient time to sell the coin before the finding of the second coin.

* Report your find to the Coroner in writing within 14 days and keep a copy of the letter. In the first instance only report the find spot as the name of the parish in which the find was made. If it is not clear which Coroner needs to be informed, ask your FLO or write to the most likely Coroner and ask for your letter to be passed on, as necessary.

* Always take photographs or have photographs taken of all possible views of all objects, before you hand the objects over. You will at least have something to show an independent valuer and, if you want to publish, there won't be any copyright or access issues.

* There is no time limit for handing over the find and you should be allowed a reasonable amount of time for such things as photographing, valuing, showing it to the landowner, displaying it at a club meeting etc. Bear in mind, however, that you are responsible for the security of the find until you hand it over.

* These days Finds Liaison Officers often collect potential treasure from finders, however you may be asked to deposit your find at a museum or FLO at your own expense. You are not legally obliged to take your find anywhere, however, if you can arrange this it is best to comply. Insist on being given the Treasure Receipt, (filled out in your presence) in exchange for your find.

* The Treasure Act Code of Practice requires that the precise find spot must be established and should be kept confidential. You can insist on the confidentiality requirement when the Treasure Receipt is completed and have the precise find spot kept separately.

* A section of the Treasure Receipt is labeled "Location of find spot". Only enter vague details of the find spot such as name of Parish, four-figure map reference or a nondescript name for the site such as 'Field A'.

* If a museum is interested in acquiring the find, a Coroner's Inquest will be arranged. You should be invited to attend the Inquest for which you can claim expenses and I suggest you should attend if you possibly can – you will at least know who was there and what was said. The press may be there, so be careful not to reveal find spot information if they are.

* Following an Inquest the Press will probably want to speak to you. Whether you speak to them is up to you but you can at least appeal for some confidentiality and perhaps avoid them uncovering, or inventing, more than you would like revealed.

* The final stumbling block is the valuation, which will be given, some weeks after the Inquest, via the British Museum, who now administer the Treasure Act. You need to know if the valuation is 'A Fair Market Value' so that you can decide whether to accept it. Fair market value is an attempt to arrive at the price you should expect to get if selling your find on the open market and the Treasure Valuation Committee tries to arrive at the 'hammer' price without auctioneer's deductions. Pick out a couple of dealers specializing in coins or objects similar to yours from the advertisements in treasure hunting magazines. Ask the dealers to give you their buying-in price for your find (send photographs if necessary). I am sure they will oblige for little or no charge. If the treasure is very rare it should be possible to arrange viewing for independent appraisal. You should be offered two opportunities to contest the valuation, one before the valuation committee meets and one after. I would accept the valuation if it falls within or above your dealers' ballpark figures and contest it if it falls below. If you are going to contest the valuation, get in before

the committee meets if you can. There is a slight possibility that the museum involved may contest the valuation and succeed in getting it reduced – if this happens, unless there is clear justification, you could appeal against it all the way to the Secretary of State, if necessary.

* An alternative is for both you and the landowner to refuse your award for the find, which will result in the find being disclaimed without inquest or valuation and being deposited in a museum. If you are very public spirited, you can make the refusal when you first report your find or alternatively wait and see if a museum is interested in acquiring the find first, as your find may be disclaimed and returned to you anyway. To refuse the award both you and the landowner should write to the Treasure Registrar at the British Museum stating your refusal, preferably before the inquest as this will save a lot of time. Of course, you can refuse the award, while the landowner keeps theirs or vice versa, in which case the museum may acquire the find at half market value or it may be disclaimed. All parties refusing awards are given a certificate of thanks.

## 2.4. Organizations, Clubs and Magazines

You may wish to metal detect alone or with a friend or two or you may prefer to join a metal detecting club for the camaraderie, help, advice and possible access to detecting land. Whichever way you continue to pursue your hobby, unless you own many acres of land yourself, you really need civil liability insurance specifically for metal detecting. This will cover you for claims made against you in the event of you causing loss or damage to someone while pursuing your hobby. Most detectorists act responsibly and claims rarely occur but accidents can and do happen. Also in the UK some landowners insist that you have such insurance as do all metal detecting rally organizers and insurance also helps to gain search permission.

### Organizations

United Kingdom detectorists can easily obtain ten million pounds insurance cover as part of the small fee for joining a national metal detecting organization. The choice is either the National Council for Metal Detecting (NCMD): General Secretary, Trevor Austin, 51 Hill Top Gardens, Denaby, DONCASTER, DN12 4SA trevor.austin@ncmd.co.uk/ http://www.ncmd.co.uk/ or the Federation of Independent Detectorists (FID): CSFID 27, Webb Road RAUNDS Wellingborough Northants NN9 6H. Website: http://fid.newbury.net/

Outside of the UK, there seems to be little in the way of similar insurance offered by metal detecting organizations, nevertheless, if there is an organization covering your locality you would be wise to join for the support and advice they can offer.

Bulgaria has the Bulgarian National Metal Detecting Federation, contact: Ilia ILIEV-President, Bulgaria, Lovech 5500 Str. "Tsar Osvoboditel" N33 Tel: +359 68 656459 http://www.metaldetecting.bg/

France has La Fédération Euoropeenne des Prospecteurs (FEP): http://prospecteur.1talk.net/ and La Fédération Nationale des Utilisateurs de Détecteurs de Métaux (FNUDEM): http://www.fnudem.net/

Netherlands has De Detector Amateur http://www.detectoramateur.nl

United States metal detectorists are represented by the Federation of Metal Detector and Archaeological Clubs (FMDAC): http://www.fmdac.org/

### Metal Detecting Clubs

Where there's a hobby there is bound to be a club and metal detecting is no exception. There are many reasons detectorists join clubs, the principal one probably being to gain access to new sites to search. But clubs offer much more for there is a great deal of expertise in the average club, which is freely passed on to new members; finds are displayed and discussed, which helps with identification and encouragement; guest speakers on various topics appear as well as there being the purely social side.

United Kingdom has around 250metal detecting clubs, which are usually affiliated to either of the aforementioned organizations: the National Council for Metal Detecting (NCMD), the largest , or the Federation of Independent Detectorists (FID), who represent a few thousand individual detectorists. More information on clubs is available from the NCMD: General Secretary, Trevor Austin, 51 Hill Top Gardens, Denaby, DONCASTER, DN12 4SA trevor.austin@ncmd.co.uk
http://www.ncmd.co.uk/regions%20and%20clubs.htm          as          well          as
http://fid.newbury.net/clubs.html                                                                  and
http://www.ukdetectornet.co.uk/clubs.html

Metal detecting is less well represented in most other European countries but there are a few clubs.

Belgium has (or had) a club called Prospector Vlaanderen http://www.archeonet.be/?p=265

Denmark has small clubs in Bornholm and Sjaeland. The main internet site is: http://www.janke.dk/detektor

France has La Fédération Euoropeenne des Prospecteurs (FEP): http://prospecteur.1talk.net/ and La Fédération Nationale des Utilisateurs de Détecteurs de Métaux (FNUDEM): http://www.fnudem.net/

Norway has a club called Norges Metallsøkerforening, Smylestrårn 4, 3261 Larvik, Norway. http://nmf.nu/

United States clubs list: http://www.goldminershq.com/clubs/metal1.htm

Worldwide links to clubs: http://gometaldetecting.com/links-clubs.htm

## Metal Detecting Magazines

France: **Detection Passion**, http://www.detectionpassion.fr/ Tel: 04.90.33.75.65. **Le Fouilleur** 63 avenue de Paris (RN.20) Boissy sous Saint Yon – 91790 http://www.lefouilleur.com/blog/ **Monnaies & Detections**, 33 boulevard Carnot 31000 Toulouse http://www.monnaiesdetections.com/

Germany: **Das Schatzsucher Magazin**, IG History, Königsstr. 16, D-61479 Glashütten, Germany. http://www.das-schatsucher-magazin-shop.de/

Italy: **MD Metal Detector**, Edizioni emmedi Via del Lavoro 4, 48015 Cervia (RA) Italy. http://www.metaldetector.it/

**Netherlands:** **The Coinhunter Magazine**, Dollard 147, 8032 KD, Zwolle, The Netherlands. http://www.thecoinhunter.com/ **Detector Magazine**, De Detector Amateur http://www.detectoramateur.nl/

**Poland: Odkrywca**, ul. Kaszubska 4 50-214 Wrocław Poland. Tel.0 71 329 71 85 or 0 71 329 71 86 http://www.odkrywca.pl

United Kingdom: **The Searcher**, 17 Down Road, Merrow, Guildford, Surrey, GU1 2PX. Tel: 01483 830133. http://www.thesearcher.co.uk/ **Treasure Hunting**, Greenlight Publishing, 119 Newland Street, Witham, Essex CM8 1WF. Tel: 01376 521900. http://www.treasurehunting.co.uk/ **UKDN Word Magazine**, the magazine of UK Detector Net, one of the oldest metal detecting sites on the Internet http://www.ukdetectornet.co.uk/word.html

United States: **American Digger Magazine** http://www.americandigger.com/ **Lost Treasure** http://losttreasure.com/ **Treasure Depot Online Magazine** http://www.thetreasuredepot.com/tdmag.html **Western & Eastern Treasures** http://www.wetreasures.com/

# 3. Equipment: Metal Detectors and Search Heads

The basic requirements for metal detecting are a metal detector, a digging implement and somewhere to store your finds safely, while detecting. There are also a number of accessories that you might consider once you have started and decided you like the hobby – these are headphones, pinpoint probe, additional search head(s) and perhaps a hand held Global Positioning System. Stout and weatherproof clothing and footwear is also important plus depending on the temperature, sunscreen, insect repellent and a water bottle.

There is an overwhelming array of metal detectors to choose from. If you already own a metal detector, then you have probably made a good choice and frankly any metal detector worth its name will perform the task reasonably well. For those of you who do not already own a metal detector, I will make a few suggestions but the final choice of what to buy must be yours. I've lost count of the number of times I've heard the question: "Which metal detector is best?" The question should really be: "Which metal detector is best for me?" For the answer depends very much on you and your requirements. How fit are you? Do you want to search beaches, rivers, farmland, underwater?

One thing to consider very carefully is the weight and balance of the detector – you can get an aching arm very quickly swinging a heavy or badly balanced detector. Hip or chest mounting the control box is an option for many detectors and it will take the weight off your arm but the box may then get in the way when you dig. I would always advise seeing and handling the metal detector before you decide to buy, which is probably best achieved by visiting one of the many specialist dealers.

The vast majority of metal detectors are designed for finding coins, jewelery and similar sized artefacts in the top few inches of ground on inland sites while discriminating out the undesirable contaminants: iron and aluminum foil, for that is what most participants of the metal detecting hobby want. Iron is a major contaminant on farmland and aluminum foil abounds on dry beaches and recreational areas. Most popular machines work on a Very Low Frequency, Transmit/Receive system, discriminate audibly and/or visually and use the motion system of ground canceling. Ground canceling nulls effects from minerals in the ground and the motion system requires the machine to be kept moving, otherwise desirable objects are also canceled out. The system actually works a lot better than might be imagined. To pinpoint a target there is usually a selectable non-motion all metal mode although it is easy enough to pinpoint in motion mode by passing the head over the target in a cross pattern. Machines at the lower end of the market may be non-motion and may have little or no discrimination although by nature, these types are fairly insensitive to iron but very sensitive to aluminum foil.

Within the motion detector range there are choices to be made regarding the desired amount of user control over the machine's electronic operation. Manufacturers are clearly split between simple 'switch on and go' and fully programmable detectors; some manufacturer's making only one type and some making both types. Logically the computer controlled programmable type will be better able to maximize depth and sort out the trash from the cash but you could spend a great deal of time messing about with the settings trying to achieve perfection instead of getting on with the searching. My own view is that if you are getting at all involved with dowsing then that will more than make up for any advantages of the computer control without the complexities but at the end of the day the choice between simplicity or bells and whistles is entirely yours. Whites has been the traditional UK choice for programmable types but C-Scope, Garrett, Minelab, XP and others also offer programmable models, with Minelab and XP leading.

A less popular type of hobby metal detector works on a principle known as pulse induction which is a non-motion (the detector signals a target whether moving or stationary) deep seeking system. These machines are notoriously sensitive to iron and very few discriminate between ferrous and non-ferrous metals (those that do discriminate tend to reject some desirable objects.) Pulse machines are firm favorites among beachcombers and underwater treasure hunters because of their ability to reach greater depths on most targets, typically twice that of many VLF machines and to cut through severe mineralization such as black sand.

There are two types of very specialized machines generally available, one being underwater detectors which are sealed to keep out water and constructed to withstand the pressures encountered in deep water. The other specialty is the so-called hoard hunters, which are usually some sort of 'two-box' design, carried like a suitcase, rather than a forearm extension as with conventional detectors. Hoard hunters are designed to find only large objects, the size of a pint (565ml) pot upwards. They do not discriminate between ferrous and non-ferrous metals as treasure may be buried in an iron container (detectors cannot usually detect through metal) and they are very deep seeking, capable of probing several feet into the ground.

**Fisher Gemini 3 hoard hunter**

The choice of machine is very much dependent on what you want to do with it. Bear in mind that as the price of detectors rise you are generally paying for more features and the increase in performance over the cheaper machine can be quite marginal. I would advise a complete novice to go for a basic machine and, all things being equal, going for one of the lower priced ones from their own Country. They are better value for money and probably more suitable for the conditions. Typically if you buy an American machine in Britain you pay pound on the dollar and the conditions and even the artefacts which are looked for are quite different in the two Countries. Consider also that if you decide not to continue with the hobby your new machine will lose around 25% of its value if you have to sell. Amongst the higher priced detectors, foreign technology may be superior to your Country's and there may be less advantage in going for the home produced model. Foreign detectors made for the British market have a large following: Laser, Minelab and Whites particularly.

With the benefit of hindsight, if I was a serious beginner in Europe, I would buy a Laser B1 or one of its successors, the Rapier or Hawkeye. To keep the cost down, I could buy used or spread the cost on interest-free credit. An alternative is to contact a local dealer and see what he recommends for you but do not be persuaded to spend a large amount of money on a bright shiny all-singing, all-dancing detector that you may well find you cannot get on with. You can always upgrade from a basic model later, when you have some experience. I am also going to stick my neck out and suggest three starter machines to consider, which I haven't personally used but they all have a good reputation: C-Scope CS1MX, Fisher F2 or Garrett Ace 150 (or 250) these are all recommended for inland sites and dry beaches only but the Garrett is also said to perform reasonably well on salt wet beaches (I haven't tried it, so check this out yourself if wet beach searching is important).

CURRENT POPULAR METAL DETECTORS

| MAKE | ORIGIN | TYPE |
|---|---|---|
| BOUNTY HUNTER | USA | VLF |
| C-SCOPE | UK | VLF |
| C-SCOPE | UK | PULSE INDUCTION |
| FISHER | USA | VLF |
| GARRETT | USA | VLF |
| LASER (TESORO) | USA FOR UK MARKET | VLF |
| MINELAB | AUSTRALIA/EIRE | VLF |
| TESORO | USA | VLF |
| VIKING | UK | VLF |
| WHITE'S | USA/UK | VLF |
| WHITE'S | USA/UK | PULSE INDUCTION |
| XP | FRANCE | VLF |

**Laser B1 metal detector**

As a general rule the more expensive the metal detector the greater the depth to which it will be able to detect buried objects but it certainly isn't twice the price equals twice the depth and depth is not everything, especially on trashy sites. If you expect to search mainly inland then a VLF machine will be most suitable. If you want to search only beaches then a pulse machine may be more suitable but bearing in mind the lack of discrimination on Pulse Induction machines, it may be preferable to go for a VLF machine with a good reputation on beaches such as Whites or Minelab.

Anyone who spends a lot of time detecting usually has more than one metal detector. I personally have four – A Detech EDS as my main machine, a Laser B1 Hi-Power as back-up and for heavily contaminated sites, a Minelab Sovereign XS2aPro, which I use mainly for beaches and a Detech SSP-3000 pulse induction for beaches and deepseeking work. I also have a selection of search heads for all machines. I wouldn't suggest that my selection represents the absolute best in metal detecting technology but, in conjunction with dowsing, it does allow me to perform well over a wide variety of sites and conditions.

## Search heads (coils)

The search head contains one or more electrical coils and while the terms head and coil are used interchangeably, here I will refer to the head as the whole unit and the coil as the internal electrical wiring. The standard search head size fitted to the majority of detectors is around eight inches (20cm) diameter, which is a compromise to enable the detector to perform reasonably well under a variety of conditions. Most manufacturers produce a range of optional search head sizes typically from 3.5" (9cm) up to 15" (38cm) diameter and these can be employed to improve performance under certain conditions. As a rule of thumb the larger the search head the deeper it will detect but they have their disadvantages too: less sensitivity to smaller targets, more difficult to use on heavily mineralized or iron contaminated ground and less accurate pinpointing. Larger search heads are also heavier and more cumbersome to use although the weight can be compensated for by hip or chest mounting the detector control box, if the machine has that facility, or by using a bungee harness.

In addition to search head size variation, there are three different types of coil construction: concentric, 2D or widescan and symmetrical electromagnetic field or SEF. Concentric coils, usually fitted to metal detectors as standard, have an inverted cone detection pattern, which achieves maximum depth only at the center of the search head. Widescan coils have a pudding basin shaped detection pattern and while they don't achieve as great a depth as the same size concentric coil they do take in a larger volume of ground per sweep. If it's fast ground coverage you are after, the widescan coil is better and if it's depth you are after the concentric coil is better. Now you can have the best of both worlds as the newly introduced symmetrical electromagnetic field or SEF coils combine both widescan and concentric coils in one.

I strongly advise that you always fit a scuff cover to protect the bottom of the search head from wearing through scraping the ground and obstructions. The scuff cover or search head protector is basically a plastic 'lid' that fits over the bottom of the search head and takes the wear and knocks. They do wear out but only cost about a tenth of the price of the search head itself to replace.

## Where to buy metal detectors and accessories

The short answer is to look through a recent metal detecting magazine for your nearest supplier or Google it as they say. Here is a list of major metal detector manufacturers and UK suppliers:

C.Scope, Kingsnorth Technology Park, Wotton Road, Ashford, Kent, TN23 6LN, Tel: 01233 629181,Website: http://www.cscope.co.uk

Crawfords Metal Detectors, F6 Mercia Way, Foxhills Industrial Estate, Scunthorpe, North Lincolnshire, DN15 8RE, Tel: 01724 845608 Email: sales@crawfordsmd.com Website: http://www.crawfordsmd.com

Detecnicks, 3 Orchard Crescent, Arundel Road, Fontwell, West Sussex, BN18 0SD, Tel: 01243 545060 Email: sales@detecnicks.co.uk Website: www.detecnicks.co.uk

Garrett Metal Detectors Website: www.garrett.com

Joan Allen Electronics Ltd, 190 Main Road, Biggin Hill, Kent, TN16 3BB Tel: 01959 571255 Email: Sales@joanallen.co.uk Website: http://www.joanallen.co.uk

Leisure Promotions, Units 6-8 Kennet Centre, Newbury, Berkshire, RG14 5EN. Tel: 01635 46040 Email: info@leisure-promotions.co.uk http://www.leisure-promotions.co.uk

Maz Detecting Supplies, 100 Ynyshir Road, Porth, Mid Glamorgan, CF39 0EW Tel: 01443 685336

Mike Longfield Detectors, 83 Station Road, Balsall Common, Nr Coventry, CV7 7FN Tel: 01676 533274 Website: http://www.metaldetectors.GBR.cc

Minelab International Limited, Unit 207, Harbour Point Business Park, Little Island, Co. Cork, Ireland Tel: 00-353-23 8852101 Website: http://www.minelab.com

Pepsi Piros Metal Detectors, 10 Carlton Road, Worksop, Nottinghamshire,S80 1PH Tel: 01909 476611 Website: http://www.metaldetectors-pepsi.co.uk/http://www.metaldetectors-pepsi.co.uk

Regton, 82 Cleveland Street, Birmingham, B19 3SN Tel: 0121 359 2379 Website: http://www.regton.com Email: sales@regton.com

Spin-A-Disc Promotions, 107 Keighley Road, Illingworth, Halifax, HX2 8JE Tel: 01422 245401 Email: sales@metaldetectingbooks.co.uk Website: http://www.metaldetectingbooks.co.uk/

Treasure World, (Laser and Tesoro Metal Detectors) P.O. Box 88, Downham Market, PE38 8BS, Tel: 07971 304050 Email: treasureworld@hotmail.co.uk Website:http://treasure-world.co.uk

Viking Metal Detectors, 1 Angela Street, Mill Hill, Blackburn, BB2 4DJ Tel: 01254 55887 Email: viking@metaldetectors.co.uk Website: http://www.metaldetectors.co.uk/

Whites Electronics (UK) Ltd, 35J Harbour Road, Inverness, IV1 1UA Tel: 01463 223456 Email: info@whites.co.uk Website: http://www.whites.co.uk

XP Metal Detectors, Website: http://www.xpmetaldetectors.co.uk/

## 3.1. Accessories

### Diggers

Detector stores probably stock nearly as many varieties of digging tools as they do metal detectors so there is something for everyone and every situation. Stainless steel tools will last longer than mild steel.

The popular general purpose digger is a small spade – a mini shovel, a junior spade, a ladies spade or a border spade. It needs to be as light as possible for carrying and reasonably pointed so you can push it into the ground easily. If it comes with a straight cutting edge then you can make it pointed with an angle grinder or find someone to do that for you. If the weight is a problem or you need a free hand you can hook it on your belt and/or drag it behind you, if necessary, but do not drag a spade over growing crops!

An alternative but not quite so good tool now that detectors are searching deeper, is a foot assisted trowel, which is purpose built for detecting. They are smaller and lighter than spades and will hang on to a belt nicely if they have a T or D shaped handle.

As the search gets into more ornamental areas like parks and gardens then digging tools need to get smaller. A strong sharp knife is very good for this but in the UK it is illegal, without a good reason, to carry a fixed or locking knife with a blade over three inches long, in a public place, which includes your car. Unfortunately, what constitutes a good reason is poorly defined and left for a magistrate to decide, so a builder's pointing trowel would be a safer alternative. It is also useful to have a Frisbee or sheet of polythene or cloth to place the removed earth on, then tip it back in the hole after recovering the find. Some metal detectorists use a blunt screwdriver around 12 inches in length to probe the ground until they hit the find and then flick it out. Personally I do not use this method as it is only really suitable for modern coinage and likely to damage finds.

**Draper mini-shovel and stainless steel sand scoop**

You can use a spade or shovel on beaches without too much difficulty although on dry sand, where the sand tends to run back into the hole, a purpose made scoop may be quicker and easier, providing the finds are not too deep. The scoop is basically a perforated, partly enclosed shovel that you push through the sand; the sand runs through the perforations leaving your find in the scoop. You could also use a plastic garden sieve. Use a shovel or large trowel to dig the hole and place the excavated sand or shingle into the sieve. Shake until only the larger objects are left and use your metal detector to sweep the sieve for metal.

For recovering finds from shallow water (most detectors are waterproof up to the underside of the control box but check this out on your detector) you can use a spade, providing the water is only a few inches deep but as the water gets deeper a long-handled scoop with drainage holes becomes almost essential. You may find a floating sieve useful, which can be made by affixing an inflated tyre inner tube around a plastic garden sieve. Do not forget to tie the sieve to you with a slack line or you will lose it. When you get a signal, dig out the sand using a scoop or spade into your sieve.

## Finds bag

Having extracted the find you need somewhere to put it safely. You might have pockets but a failing pocket may have been responsible for the loss of the find in the first place so you really need a finds bag. The type I prefer is the apron type, similar to those worn by market traders for holding their cash, again available from most metal detector retailers. Those that I use have four deep pockets: the front two being open and the rear two zipped. Being right-handed I use the right front pocket for trash; the right rear pocket for sturdy finds; the left front pocket for polythene bags, marker, etc. and the left rear pocket to keep any fragile, important or easily damaged finds, each in its own bag.

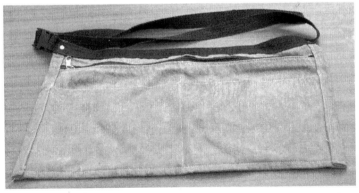

**Finds bag**

## Headphones

Most detectorists, including myself, consider headphones to be essential for they not only cut out background noise and allow you to hear the fainter signals from smaller and/or deeper objects but they cut out the detector's internal speaker, using less power and prolonging battery life. Headphones also work the other way in muffling noise from the detector which makes you less invasive to other people and wildlife. There are several good headphones built especially for metal detectors, such as Maz, although they can be quite expensive. In my opinion it is worth paying the money as they are far superior to ordinary high fidelity headphones and last much longer. Generally they have volume control and the ability to switch between mono and stereo to suit different detectors.

## Pinpoint probe

An extremely useful accessory is an electronic pinpoint probe, a miniature metal detector, available from most metal detector dealers. This gadget helps identify the exact position of the find in the hole so you can not only avoid damage but speed up find extraction considerably. Probes with a limited range, perhaps no more than an inch on a small object, can be bought from metal detector dealers for a few pounds. There is now a new breed of pulse induction probes like the Garrett Pro-Pointer which have a much greater range and a larger price tag but they are so much better at pinpointing than the old style probes and well worth the money.

**Garrett Pro-Pointer**

## Portable mapping

There are many benefits from keeping track of find spots. Metal objects are mainly lost where human beings were active in the past, which creates 'hot spots' that will yield numerous coins and artefacts relating to the period of activity. By logging your find spots you will see patterns emerging that will lead to more good finds and may add interest to your searches as the picture of past human activity develops. Most landowners are intensely interested in the finds from their land and like to know, at least, what was found, where it was found and why it was there in the first place. By answering as many of their questions as you can, you will endear yourself to the landowner with obvious benefits.

If your find happens to be classed as potential treasure (see Chapter: 2.3, The Treasure Act) then there is a requirement to supply an accurate find spot. While this is not strictly mandatory, the Treasure Act Code of Practice does imply that awards could be reduced for failing to identify the find spot. Finally, the Portable Antiquities Scheme has set up a network of Finds Liaison Officers and a database for recording finds (mainly over 300 years old) made by the public. Reporting is entirely voluntary and must be with the landowner's permission, however I feel we should report finds to the PAS if we possibly can – it is good for the hobby in that we are giving information back for what we are taking away.

Many detectorists seem to have developed a photographic memory as far as memorizing where objects were found and if you have such a memory then perhaps you need do nothing more than record your finds on a map, in a notebook or database when you get home from detecting. If you do not have such a good memory, probably the best way to record finds in the field is to place significant finds in numbered polythene bags cross-referenced to a map or Global Positioning System. At this stage you can use any small polythene bags between about 3inches (7.5cm) square to about 8inches (20cm) square that can be closed to prevent the find falling out. You can get small sealable polythene bags from most stationers or use bank coin bags (as long as the finds don't need to be kept wet). The polythene bags need to be numbered with a suitable permanent marker which you can do before you go out detecting or take the marker with you and number the bags as you make the finds. Permanent markers with bullet points are easier to write with than the alternative chisel points.

I don't suppose you really want to carry large maps around with you in the field, however a cheap and effective alternative is to use a credit card wallet and make copies of maps or sketches of the fields you are searching on cards which you keep in the wallet. When you make a significant find you pop it in a numbered bag and use a fine tipped permanent marker to mark the find spot on the map card.

The highly technical method of find spot recording is to use a hand held Global Positioning System (GPS). In the 1970s the United States Defense Department developed GPS so that military units would know their own and other units exact location anywhere on the planet. The system works by means of 24 satellites orbiting the earth and arranged so that at least six satellites are transmitting their position and time data to any point in the world. Portable or hand-held receivers collect the satellite data and determine the instrument's exact location, elevation, speed and time, 24 hours a day regardless of the weather. GPS is being increasingly used in cars, boats and planes, where it is more usually called satellite navigation or 'satnav' and is free for anyone to use, you just have to buy a receiver, which are now fairly modestly priced and not much bigger than a cell phone.

GPS is almost unbelievably accurate to within a few metres, which is extremely useful for plotting find spots, especially as the receiver can determine location by Ordnance Survey grid reference in Britain. I have a Garmin eTrex H, using which I'll describe how to record a find spot. It is very simple. At the beginning of your detecting session you would normally switch the unit on and wait a minute or two for the receiver to lock on to the satellites. When you have dug a find you want to log, you stand on the find spot and toggle through the pages to the menu page and enter 'mark'. The next sequential number is displayed with the Grid Reference and 'OK?' Enter again and the find spot is logged until you delete it. To recall the find spot you toggle through the pages to the menu page. Enter 'waypoints'. The list is displayed which you toggle through to the find spot you want and read it off for recording on your map or database or you can navigate your way back to it. The Garmin eTrex H can store up to 500 find spots, which it will retain until you delete them regardless of being switched on or off.

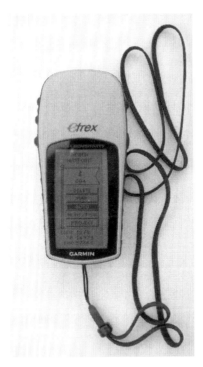

**GPS: find spot marked at OS TR14979 57865**

## Basic washing

While it is not considered good practice to wash or clean a find in the field, I do carry some basic washing equipment with me on my forays, which I leave in the car. The reason for this is that although I have the will-power to wait until I get home before doing anything with a find, on a couple of occasions I have found potential treasure which I have needed to show to the landowner and his family on the spot. There is a great temptation here for people to try and rub the dirt off, which could do great damage to the object, particularly if it is gold. It is much better to carefully wash the find before allowing it to be handled by others. So my washing kit consists of a travel dog bowl with integral water supply (from a pet store), a soft toothbrush and a small plastic sieve or tea strainer to hold the find and catch anything important that might be washed off. It also serves for washing hands before lunch, al fresco.

## Spare batteries

Always carry a spare set of batteries as you will often be detecting far way from shops. If you are going a long way from your car or base, take the batteries with you but not loose in your pocket as they can short out, discharge and even cause a fire. The original packaging or a small plastic box is best for carrying batteries in the field.

## Clothing and footwear

Shoes or trainers will soon wear out, so you really need stout footwear such as walking boots or wellington boots (especially for wetter conditions). Avoid steel toecaps and steel reinforced arches unless safety footwear is required on the site you are working (extend your detector stem to maximum length here to keep the search head away from your feet). I always wear an extra pair of thick socks for greater comfort, whatever the season, although I tend to wear thermal socks in winter.

You will need a variety of clothing to suit the climate but most of it you should be able to source from your wardrobe or even a charity shop. I wear casual work-wear trousers all year round; some wear jeans and others wear shorts in summer. I do not normally wear shorts for metal detecting as it leaves bare legs exposed to scratches, insect bites and sunburn. I wear a long sleeved tee shirt or polo shirt in summer as I find the detector arm cup tends to rub bare skin. As the temperature drops I will change to a sweat shirt then add a body warmer and finally a wind and waterproof coat. I also have a waterproof PVC jacket and over trousers in the car in case I am caught out in wet weather. I always wear a baseball type cap to prevent sunburn in summer and heat loss in winter.

I only used to wear gardening type gloves during winter to keep my hands warm and usually found them a bit of a nuisance when picking up small finds and had to keep taking one off. Recently I was introduced to Lycra industrial gloves with latex waterproof grip undersides, which I now wear all year round as protection against many nasty things I may encounter in the great outdoors. They are not really warm enough to wear on their own in winter so I still wear gardening gloves on top but I now only need to take the top glove off to deal with some finds. Some detectorists like to wear surgical gloves as protection against farm chemicals and animal deposits and I note that a range of industrial strength re-usable nitrile gloves is now available and ideal for this purpose.

I always wear (safety) glasses when detecting – either photochromic (Reactolite) glasses, which darken in sunlight or sunglasses on bright days and clear glasses on dull days. Apart from protecting your eyes from the sun, glasses will also protect your eyes from kamikaze insects and dust and debris that is kicked up in the course of detecting. Other items I find essential at warmer times of the year are suntan lotion, insect repellent and bottled water.

Finally, it is a good idea to ensure your Tetanus immunization is up to date. Jagged and sharp metal abounds in fields and beaches and any resulting wounds can be infected by Tetanus bacteria, which thrive outdoors.

40

## 3.2. How to Use a Metal Detector

Today's metal detectors are well-engineered and the actual operating controls are usually very easy and simple to operate. However, once you have your metal detector you should read and then re-read the instruction manual. If you have acquired a used detector and don't have the manual, they are usually freely available on the Internet or you can contact the manufacturer or agent.

On typical detectors the search head contains two coils. One transmits a signal into the ground and the other coil receives the signal. The coils are designed so that the signal currents exactly balance. When the search head passes over a metal object a change of balance is induced and the receiving signal current increases. This increase is detected by the electronics in the control box and converted into an audible 'beep' (and visual indication, if fitted).

It is important to remember that the electric field generated by the search head does not only go down into the ground, it also rises above the head to the same extent as below and travels out from the edges a somewhat shorter distance. You may get signals from metal above ground such as fences or steel reinforced concrete walls. Fixed metal on your detector such as the stem or a search head retaining bolt are discriminated out and ignored but beware of any moving metal like a slack cable. Please note that, while the search head cable needs to be wrapped fairly tightly around the stem, you do need to leave some flexibility at the search head end so that the head can move, without straining the cable or joint with the head, when it hits the many obstructions you will encounter and which could result in a costly search head replacement. On that very point, always fit a scuff cover to prevent the search head from wearing out.

Most detectors are of the motion type, which means they cancel the adverse effect of minerals in the ground by the search head being constantly moved, albeit slowly. This means if you hold the search head still over a detected object the object will be canceled too.

Having thoroughly read and re-read the manual you should now know how to put your machine together, adjust it for your height and how to switch it on. Probably the next thing to get to grips with is how to sweep. The search head should be held horizontal to the ground at a height of one to two inches or two to five centimetres above the ground, avoiding any obvious obstructions. Remember that for every inch or centimetre the search head is above the ground, there is an equivalent loss of depth below ground. The best way to use a detector is to sweep smoothly in a comfortable, roughly 90 degree arc, from in front of your feet to straight out from your side, which will help keep the head flat relative to the ground.

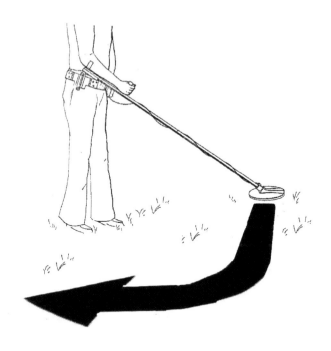

## Sweeping the detector

A common mistake is to lift the search head like a pendulum at the ends of the sweep, which results in missed finds where the head lifts off the ground. To cover the ground thoroughly always overlap sweeps and work slowly. The degree of overlap needed is dependent on the pattern in which the electric field is emitted from the search head. An inverted cone pattern only detects at maximum depth in a very small area in the centre of the search head so may warrant only an advance of a couple of inches or a few centimetres at a time otherwise you will be putting a sawtooth detection pattern into the ground and missing finds between the 'teeth'. Widescan search heads are more forgiving and an advance of about half the search head diameter at each sweep should be sufficient to maximize ground coverage. Another factor is that the way an object is orientated may prevent it being detected from one particular direction and it would be prudent to go over the same piece of ground at right angles to the first search.

When you start detecting a new site it usually pays to wander over it to sample and get a feel for what is there. Pay particular attention to bumps, dips, large trees, corners and varying soil coloration. For a more formal sampling technique you could search what becomes a multiple diamond and triangle pattern (see diagram). That is, starting in the bottom left corner, detect along the bottom boundary to the right corner, over to the top left corner, along the top boundary to the right corner, return to the bottom left corner, detect half way up the left boundary, then across to the mid-point of the right boundary, finally detect mid-point to mid-point until you have gone completely around the site. Of course sites are rarely a regular shape but the basic search pattern can be still used regardless or you can sub-divide the site into a number of rectangles, which you treat individually. When you have made your initial search, undoubtedly you will find some part or parts of the search area are more productive than others and it may be worthwhile concentrating on the more productive parts, especially if you only have access to the site for short periods.

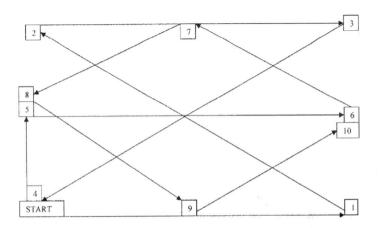

**Suggested initial site search pattern**

To ensure maximum coverage when searching an area, you can use lines and pins to mark out strips the width of a detector sweep. However, with the normal four prong search technique you will find you lose much detecting time by running up and down moving at least one of the lines to create the next search strip. I have a solution using three 10-12 inch heavy duty plastic tent pegs, which I call the three prong search technique.

43

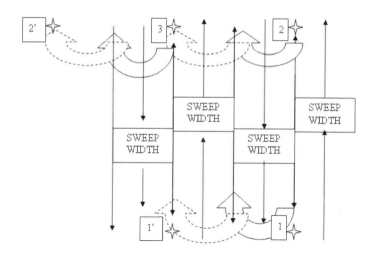

**Three prong search technique (detector in right hand)**

Having mentally defined your search area:

* Start in the right-hand corner if you use your detector in your right-hand or the left-hand corner if you use your detector in your left hand.

* Place peg no.1 in the ground at the outside of your left foot if your detector is in your right hand or the outside of your right foot if your detector is in your left hand.

* Detect forward in a straight line for about twenty yards (which is a reasonable length to keep in line with the pegs) and place peg no.2 in the ground at the outside of the same foot as previously.

* Turn round 180 degrees beside peg no.2, and make a full comfortable sweep to your side with your metal detector. While still outstretched, place the search head on the ground and walk around your detector search head to arrive at a comfortable sweep length the other side of it and place peg no.3 in the ground at the outside of the same foot as previously.

* Return to peg no.2 and search, retracing your footsteps, back to peg no.1.

* Stand beside peg no.1, pick the peg up and make a full comfortable sweep to your side with your metal detector. Placing the search head on the ground, walk around your detector search head to arrive at a comfortable sweep length the other side of it and place peg no.1 in the ground (1' in diagram).

* Search in a straight line back to peg no.3 and retrieve peg no.2. Return to peg no 3 and facing peg no 1', make a full comfortable sweep to your side with your metal detector. While still outstretched, place the search head on the

44

ground and walk around your detector search head to arrive at a comfortable sweep length the other side of it and place peg no.2' in the ground at the outside of the same foot as previously.

* Return to peg no.3 and search, retracing your footsteps, back to peg no.1'.

* Just keep repeating the steps, moving the single peg 1 across two sweeps (sweep and walk around the search head) every time you reach it and retrieving and moving the furthest away of the two pegs across two sweeps every time you reach one of them.

This may sound a little complicated but once you get used to it, it will help you cover ground thoroughly without the hassle of using lines and pins.

Different metals make slightly different sounds when detected and experience can tell you which is which to some extent. Most metal detectors have the option to variably discriminate between non-ferrous metals (such as aluminum, copper, gold, lead, silver and zinc) and ferrous (iron) metal like most nails. Most detectors can also discriminate against aluminum foil or silver paper. Because of the huge variety of sizes and shapes of metal objects, discrimination is far from perfect and needs to be used with care or you could also reject or ignore desirable and valuable objects like gold rings. Most experienced metal detectorists use as little discrimination as possible.

Dig all targets until you become experienced and can distinguish between the different 'tones' and 'beeps' of different metals and objects. Don't assume that what you hear is just another drinks can or rusty nail. Undoubtedly you will often be disappointed with what you dig up but the thrill and enjoyment of finding something lost or buried perhaps over 3000 years ago will more than make up for many disappointments.

Most metal detectors available today will locate small metal objects like coins to a depth of between six inches or 15cm and about a foot or 30cm and larger metal objects to a depth of about three feet or one metre. Your metal detector's ability to signal the presence of an object will change depending on soil and other conditions. Ground mineralization is a major factor, which can more than halve the depth that the same object can be detected in air. Ground compaction is another major factor, cultivation puts air into the soil, expanding the soil layer so metal objects are effectively deeper than when the soil is compacted. Moisture in the ground is yet another factor; metal objects can be detected deeper when the ground is damp. The condition and orientation of the object in the ground can also make a marked difference. For example a coin that is buried vertically on edge presents a much smaller surface area to the metal detector and will be more difficult to find than a coin which is lying horizontally flat.

## Pinpointing your find

Once you have learned how to use your detector, the next issue is extracting your find from its resting-place without damage – I can't imagine anything worse than having a nice find ruined by being hit with a digging tool. If your detector has a pinpoint mode it is advisable to use it to identify the position of your find in the ground as closely as possible before you start digging. Metal detectors vary on pin-point accuracy and only experience will tell you how big a diameter hole you need to dig to avoid striking the find. Start with a generously large diameter, say the size of your search head and only reduce it as you gain experience over time.

The most popular way of pin-pointing is to pass the search head over the find in a cross pattern and your find will be at the centre of the cross. This is actually achieved, once your detector signals, by sweeping your search head over the find and mentally determining the point where the signal is loudest. You can physically mark the centre by digging your heel into the ground at that point or making a mental note of any natural indicator like a stone. Turn yourself through 90 degrees so that you are at right angles to your first sweep, then sweep and find the loudest signal again, which should coincide with your mark from the first sweep. The find will be more or less below your mark. This method works well for standard-sized search heads, particularly those with concentric coils. For larger search heads and widescan or symmetrical electromagnetic field (SEF) coils there is another method you can use, called the wiggle method.

If you want to use the wiggle method, once your detector signals a find, sweep the search head back towards yourself until you lose the signal. Put your foot in place of the search head so that your toe is in line with the front of the search head, which can be easily achieved by placing your foot alongside the search head and gently moving the search head out of the way with your foot. Push your digger into the ground immediately in front of your toe, then turn through 90 degrees and relocate the find. Back the search head off again and dig into the ground again at the front of the search head where you lost the signal. Bearing in mind that the find must always be in front of where you lost the signal, you have now effectively marked a semi-circle around the find so you can now circle around the find and dig it out.

Dig out the ground one shovelful or trowelful at a time and place it at the side of the hole, then pass your metal detector search head over both hole and removed spoil. You will then know if your find is still in the hole or in the spoil. If you still get a signal from the hole then dig out more spoil and keep checking with your metal detector until your find is out of the hole. Once your find is in the spoil you can divide the spoil up into progressively smaller lots checking for the find with your metal detector. Often you can do this by grabbing handfuls of spoil and passing one handful at a time over the search head until you get a signal but make sure you are not wearing rings or a watch or bracelet on your wrist.

I find the new PI probes invaluable for extracting finds quickly, easily and without damage and urge you to add one to your kit as soon as possible. You can check the surface for shallow finds even before you dig and can usually identify exactly where your find is by checking inside the hole with the probe.

Once you have found and removed your metal object search the hole again with your metal detector. And don't forget to search the spoil you have removed from the hole. The first item you find may be just one item from a hoard and it is very often the case that where you find one object you will find more.

The most important point is that you absolutely must work tidily. There is little point in making the effort of getting permission only to have it withdrawn because you are making a mess and putting the whole hobby into disrepute as well. So wherever you are searching – field, beach, garden – you must leave the site as you found it with all holes filled in and extracted rubbish removed. If the land is used by domestic animals such as livestock or horses the consequences of leaving unfilled holes could be tragic. King William III was killed when his horse stepped into a small hole – fortunately there were no metal detectors in 1702, so they can't blame us for that.

Landscaped areas such as gardens and parks need special attention and you should aim for invisible extractions. On lawns and in parks, use a straight-edged trowel to cut a neat plug with three or four sides approximately 200mm (8″) long. Cut the plug with sloping sides to help its keying in when you replace it. Lift out the plug, invert it and place it and any other soil you extract on a sheet of polythene, plastic bag, cloth or Frisbee so that loose dirt and the plug can be put back into the hole, the same way it came out, without leaving a brown halo on the surrounding grass. In very dry weather the grass will die back after being disturbed, so either water the grass after extracting the find (you may need to carry a bottle of water with you for this purpose) or only search these places when the ground is damp.

On pasture and rough grassland you can probably dispense with the dirt collecting devices and just put everything back in the hole in the reverse order that it came out, then brush away any loose soil with your foot into the surrounding grass. But do not leave metal junk or stones on the surface to injure animals or damage mowing machinery.

On disturbed land such as ploughed fields and beaches refilling the hole and removing extracted junk will suffice. Some farmers may allow you to detect on growing crops and in this case you must replant any disturbed crop, green side up!

## Starting out

The best way to start is in your garden or that of an accommodating relative or friend, if you don't have your own. Ideally you want to make a test bed. Start by using your detector in all-metal or minimum discrimination to clear a reasonably large open area. You should also practice your finds extraction technique. When you have a suitable area clear of metal bury a selection of different coins and other metal objects such as ring pull tabs, iron nails, silver paper, drinks cans etc. Bury similar objects at different depths and also bury coins in a vertical as well as a horizontal position. Bear in mind that some modern coins (UK 1p, 2p since 1992; 5p, 10p since 2012) and drinks cans are plated steel (check with a magnet which sticks to steel) and these will signal very differently, if at all, compared to their non-ferrous counterparts. You can then work your detector over the test bed at various settings and get used to the different sounds of different metals at different depths.

Elsewhere in this book you will find outlined numerous productive sites where you can find interesting and possibly valuable coins and artefacts. Wherever you search always make sure you leave the site in the condition you found it and don't destroy anything in your enthusiasm to find treasure.

# 4. Gaining Search Permission

The biggest problems facing the treasure hunting and metal detecting hobbies today are undoubtedly finding productive land and securing search permission. Research in itself will always help secure search permission by effectively answering the landowner's question: Why do you want to search my land? What's more you are almost guaranteed good finds once you obtain permission. So site research (see chapter 6) is a very good way of improving your chances of obtaining permission.

As the new chairman of a metal detecting club, which over the years had become a 'landless society', I was charged with the task of finding land for the club to search. This is where things can get difficult. Many landowners will willingly give permission to one or two detectorists to search but facial contours distort somewhat when you say: "And will it be OK if I bring twenty mates along?" I skirt around this problem for the club by saying 'as few as one or two of us' and if that is the agreement then the club can run a rota system so that all can share eventually in the 'reduced number searches'. One other potential problem with clubs is the amount of cars that turn up for a search. Car sharing doesn't seem to go down well with detectorists and this can be a problem for a farmer. Please make sure it isn't a problem or you probably won't be visiting that farm again.

Let's now take a look at the reasons search permissions are refused. The biggest reason used to be the non-committal: "We don't allow that sort of thing." Today, in my area, Kent, the most often quoted reason is that: we already have a couple of detectorists on our land. As well as still not allowing that sort of thing, another reason might be that the occupier is a tenant and in that case, the tenant will usually co-operate if you get permission from the landowner.

Our task is not to try and oust other detectorists from land they have diligently obtained permission to search and any attempts at that may result in everyone being banned from that particular land. But rather to work around other detectorists' patches by seeking out productive land where permission can be relatively easily obtained or no other detectorist treads, for whatever reason.

When you gain search permission, it is a good idea to have a written agreement. Most landowners, however, seem to prefer verbal agreements and you will just have to go along with that if that is the case. Occasionally a landowner will insist on a written agreement, so there is one you can use later in this chapter.

## Tracking down landowners

It always helps a great deal when seeking search permission if you can address your request to the landowner by name. If nothing else it shows you have done your homework.

The easiest place to start is the classified section of the telephone directory, which in the UK are: http://www.192.com Yellow Pages; http://www.yell.com Thompsons; http://www.thomsonlocal.com etc. You can get access to printed directories outside of your telephone area at your local library and online directories cover the entire UK. A typical search would be for farmers in a locality, defined by name of nearest town or city or first half of postcode. If you have more information such as name of farm, address, etc. you may be able to perform a more selective search.

There are a couple of points here. The entry does not necessarily list the name of the current landowner, some farms have business names and those with personal names may date from the nineteenth century or even earlier. For farms with personal names, if you can't get any closer to the current landowner's name, then if you use Mr. (surname) you will be OK much of the time. For farms having business names you could address letters to the landowner or chief executive and start: Dear Sir. However this is not very satisfactory and you would be better to pursue other avenues to find the name of the landowner. The second point is that the names and addresses of these farms are public knowledge and many detectorists in the area have probably already tried them, so if you are approaching them without a good reason, expect to be turned down.

Another method of finding the landowner, particularly useful for fields with no obvious farmhouse attached is to visit the area and ask people living or working in the immediate vicinity. You could also ask at the local church, local shops or businesses, post office, newsagent or public house.

## Writing a letter and getting it read

If you have the ability to knock on any landowner's door for the first time and sweet talk him or her into unconditional permission, please carry on! For most of us, it is a very different story and writing is usually the best way to avoid being traumatized or getting a flea in the ear. Writing has the advantage of introducing yourself and your hobby at the recipient's leisure, giving him a chance for a considered reply, rather than a knee-jerk no! If the landowner feels strongly negative, then a quick note returned to that effect avoids a potentially unpleasant confrontation. Some landowners will respond positively almost immediately but the majority will not respond at all and you won't know why, at the time. This is the downside of letter writing.

One reason for lack of response could be that your letter was never read. This may be because your letter is illegible or unintelligible or was never received or not opened. We can and should take steps to maximize the chances of our letter being read.

Firstly a hand written letter will probably be the best received, providing it is completely and easily readable. You should know how well you own penmanship is received, if not, ask anyone who does not know your writing well to assess an example. If there is any doubt, you must type or word-process your letters, or have someone do that for you.

Business type letter headings are best avoided although club letter headings are generally acceptable. A typical letter might be laid out as the example on the next page. Save your letter if you have produced it on a word processor, otherwise make a copy of the letter and keep it.

Put the letter in an envelope with minimal folding. Enclose a first-class stamped self-addressed envelope, a copy of the Code of Practice and copies of maps and any other printed material that supports your argument for wanting to search the land. Indicate on the map where you want to search if it isn't obvious. Affix postage stamps to the correct first-class postage rate. Avoid labels or franking as this may make your letter look like a circular and get it relegated to the bin.

Post the letter and wait. You will often get a fairly quick yes. If you haven't heard from the landowner by the end of four weeks, visit him, if possible, taking a copy of your letter and any research with you. You are not 'cold calling' so he should be approachable and you will just have to try and convince him to say yes even if it is only for a short probationary period.

If you can't get to see the landowner send another brief letter suggesting you think the first may have been lost in the post and enclose duplicates of everything you previously sent.

<u>Properly addressed?</u>

I well remember passing finds around a dining table large enough to seat a couple of football teams, when I was invited in for tea and cake by a Knight and his Lady. Metal detecting is a very interesting hobby and you often find yourself having to write or speak to all manner of people – aristocracy, clergy, businessmen – and many have strong preferences as to how they are addressed. While it is not a criminal offence to get it wrong, it will help your case greatly if you get it right.

In my book, **Permission Impossible**, I cover the most likely 'titled' persons you are likely to come across and generally include the correct address for the envelope, the letter opening (Dear:) and how they should be addressed if you need to speak to them. If I haven't covered the situation or you don't have my book, you will need to get down to your local library and consult one of the following books:

**Burke's Peerage and Baronetage**

**Debrett's Peerage and Baronetage**

**Pears' Cyclopaedia**

**Titles and Forms of Address**, (A&C Black)

Webster, Jennifer, **Forms of Address for Correspondence and Conversation**

**Whitaker's Almanack**

## Writing to businesses

Farmers are the most likely businesses you will be dealing with and they are often either one-man-bands or family businesses, so if you have a name, address your letter to that person. With any business you deal with it is always better to try and find out the name of the person who deals with matters relating to company land and how they like to be addressed (Dr., Mr., Mrs., Ms., Miss, etc). A quick phone call to the business concerned will usually establish that and unless it is a very small business you shouldn't get dragged into a conversation about the precise nature of your interest in their land. If you must write without the person's details, address your letter to The Secretary and start your letter: Dear Sirs.

When signing off the letter, if you don't know the addressees name and you start your letter Dear Sirs, it is safest to use: 'Yours faithfully'. Use: 'Yours sincerely', if you address your letter to someone by name. Similarly when writing to titled people other than directly to Royalty or the Pope use: 'Yours sincerely', if you know the person personally or 'Yours faithfully', if you don't.

52

## Example letters

Your name

Your address

Your telephone number

Your email address (if you have one)

(Date)

(Landowner's title) (Landowner's Surname)

(Landowner's Address)

Dear (Title e.g. Mr) (Surname),

Several years ago a local farmer (name, if possible) kindly gave me permission to use a metal detector on his land. The finds recovered, from the top few inches of soil (coins, tokens, buttons, buckles and a variety of other metal artefacts that had been lost, hidden or discarded over the past 2000 years) led me to develop a considerable interest in the history of the area.

During the course of research I have come across several references to a Roman road that is supposed to have run through (name) parish. According to major sources (e.g. Ordnance Survey Map of Roman Britain) the road ran from the Iron working area of (name) through (name) to (name), where it crossed the river and traveled up the east side to (name). It looks highly probable that the road continued on from (name) to (name) Street, crossing your land. It is, perhaps, worth noting that Roman finds have been made on nearly all adjoining fields.

I would greatly appreciate having your permission to use a metal detector on your land with a view to determining the course of the Roman road.

In return for your kind permission, I would offer to:

1. Report all worthwhile finds and findings to you.

2. Share any finds or their value with you on the customary 50/50 basis.

3. Work tidily without leaving a mess; removing all junk uncovered.

4. Respect your property and take care to avoid causing damage, loss or hindrance (I have N.F.U./C.L.A. approved Public Liability Insurance).

5. Abide by any conditions that you may wish to impose.

I am at your disposal should you require further information or a demonstration and look forward to your reply.


Yours Sincerely,


(Your Signature)


(Your Name)

Enc: SAE, Code of Practice, blank search agreement, copies of any maps or research documents


The example above presupposes that you already have permission on some farmland (it always helps if a landowner has already given you permission). If you are seeking land for the first time a more suitable letter might read:

If, like me, you have an interest in the history of (parish) you will probably know that the village used to host an annual fair. I have a copy of Owen's book of fairs dated 1773 which states the fair was held on July 25 for edge tools. At the time, everyone seemed to know how to find the fair from just the village name so the site of the fair is not recorded.


(Then explain why you think the fair or whatever was held on their land)


I would greatly appreciate having your permission to use a metal detector on your land to recover metal objects, such as coins, tokens, buttons and buckles, from the top few inches of soil to determining if the (event) was held there.

In return for your kind permission, I would offer to:

1. Report all worthwhile finds and findings to you.

2. Share any finds or their value with you on the customary 50/50 basis.

3. Work tidily without leaving a mess; removing all junk uncovered.

54

4. Respect your property and take care to avoid causing damage, loss or hindrance (I have N.F.U./C.L.A. approved Public Liability Insurance).

5. Abide by any conditions that you may wish to impose.

I am at your disposal should you require further information or a demonstration and look forward to your reply.


Yours Sincerely,


(Your Signature)


(Your Name)

Enc: SAE, Code of Practice, blank search agreement, copies of any maps or research documents

# Landowner/Searcher Agreement

The following terms and conditions are agreed between landowner and searcher:

The landowner grants permission to the searcher to use location equipment and hand tools to search and extract finds from the ground of land known as:

................................................................................................

................................................................................................

During the period: **From:**.......................... **To:**...............................

The searcher enters the land at the searcher's own risk.

The searcher shall report all worthwhile finds to the landowner within a reasonable time of being found in accordance with the landowner's wishes.

The searcher shall report any bombs, missiles or live ammunition discovered, to the landowner and to the police.

Archaeological discoveries will be reported to the landowner in the first instance. The information can then be passed on to the, Portable Antiquities Scheme, local museum or archaeological body according to the landowner's wishes.

Potential treasure discoveries will be reported to the landowner in the first instance providing this can be achieved within fourteen days. The searcher will carry out any mandatory legal reporting obligations.

All finds (or the value thereof) and treasure awards will be shared equally between the searcher and landowner.

The searcher shall take great care to: work tidily, avoid hindrance to the working of the land and avoid damage to the landowner's, property, animals or crops. In the unlikely event of damage the searcher shall rectify the damage at the searcher's own expense.

The searcher shall comply with any special conditions, recorded overleaf.

This agreement may be terminated by the landowner at any time and if so terminated the searcher shall immediately cease all operations.

|  | SEARCHER: | LANDOWNER: |
|---|---|---|
| NAME: | | |
| ADDRESS: | | |
| SIGNATURE | | |
| DATE: | | |

56

# 5. How and Where to Search

Get out and search. Equip yourself with clothing and footwear to cope with all but the most hostile weather conditions and include a waterproof cover for your metal detector in your kit (or at least a plastic bag or shower cap). Build yourself a portfolio of different types of sites so that you have sites available, which can be searched throughout the year. Metal detecting sites you can consider are: allotments, arable land, beaches, building sites, camp sites, footpaths, river foreshores, gardens, meadows, orchards, parkland, pasture, set-a-side, watercourses and woodland. Arable land is often only available for a few weeks in autumn or spring, whereas beaches, foreshores and watercourses can be searched all year round. Orchards are generally searchable between autumn and spring, while pasture and woodland should be searchable most of the year.

Check the weather forecast before you go out, there are plenty of on line weather forecasts available such as http://www.bbc.co.uk/weather Other than that, there are a couple of useful old rhymes, which are uncannily accurate.

Red sky at night, shepherds' delight

Red sky in the morning, shepherds take warning


If it rains before seven [a.m.] it will be dry by eleven [a.m.]

If it rains after two [p.m.] it will rain the day through

## 5.1. Water Sites

### Beach and foreshore

While beaches and tidal river foreshores have been in use for thousands of years for gathering food, fishing and the launching and landing of boats, the seventeenth century saw an upsurge in the number of beach users owing to the practice of sea bathing for perceived health benefits. Following a rise in popularity during the eighteenth century, thousands of people have visited beaches every year to enjoy boating, playing games, sunbathing, swimming, relaxing and having fun. Even today, the majority of families have at least one of their annual holidays on a beach somewhere. Trains, motor transport and the airplane made it increasingly possible for families to travel long distances to resorts and many beaches, particularly in warmer climes, are packed with people all through the summer.

Over the centuries thousands of ships have been wrecked off coasts around the World, particularly off shale and rock beaches where the seas can be very treacherous. Many ships sank with huge quantities of treasure and valuables including Spanish galleons which sank with vast hoards of gold and silver over 400 years ago. Tides, winds and storms often deposit this treasure, particularly gold and silver coins, on the beach. Most modern metal detectors can be used in a couple of feet of water to search for these treasures and there are also metal detectors available especially for searching under water.

Not only are beaches well visited by people but beach activities positively encourage metal objects to be lost. In hot weather, rings become slightly larger and slide off fingers; in sea water fingers get smaller and rings slide off. Sun-tan lotion acts as a lubricant, aiding ring slippage, while swimming and frolicking puts a strain on the catches of neck chains and bracelets, which are also frequently lost. One source quotes over 20,000 rings are lost annually, just on British beaches. Most jewelery is never found by its owners. Rarely do people know exactly where they lost anything and even if they did, it is still extremely difficult to find without a metal detector. Jewelry and coins are also lost playing beach games, while trouser and shorts pockets were not designed to safely retain coins and valuables when their wearers are lounging in deck chairs. People going bathing in the sea habitually leave their valuables behind in a towel or removed clothes, then absent-mindedly tip them into the sand when drying off and dressing.

Beaches and tidal river foreshores make excellent search areas but you should always be extremely careful when metal detecting and be aware of the ever changing conditions and the high and low tides. Always make sure that you have an easy and preplanned route back to safety if the tide is rising. Protect your detector from wind-blown sand and spray by fitting a waterproof cover to the control box and other exposed electronic units. You can usually buy manufactured control box covers or get by with elasticized shower caps or plastic bags held on with rubber bands.

You will maximize the amount of beach available and your search time if you arrive, when the beach is not crowded, roughly three hours before low tide. You should then be able to productively search until three hours after low tide. You can best find the state of the tide from local annual tide tables bought very cheaply from angling stores or chandlers. Local coastal newspapers also print daily or weekly tide tables. On the Internet you can just Google tide times with place name and you will be directed to a website like http://www.tidetimes.org.uk which will provide the information. You can also get an App like 'Tides Near Me' for your smart phone or tablet.

The tide cycle, that is the period from one low tide to the next low tide or one high tide to the next high tide, is roughly 12.5 hours. Tidal movement is not even; the water rises or falls fastest at mid-tide and slowest at low and high tides. The range of the tide and by the same token beach coverage and exposure is maximized on spring tides around the time of full moon and new moon and minimized on neap tides around the time of the two quarter moons. Phases of the moon are usually given in tide tables and diaries, pictorially represented as a black circle for new moon, white circle for full moon and either a crescent or a black and white circle for each of the two quarters.

You could use your metal detector anywhere and everywhere on beaches and you will make finds, particularly if you fit the largest search head you can handle on to your metal detector, so you cover the beach fast. There are, however, several areas which may prove more rewarding than others for finding mainly modern losses.

Areas where money changes hands

Deck chair rental points and concession stands like children's rides, food, drinks, ice cream, etc. where people gather or queue, are excellent places to search. The sites of abandoned concession sites will also hold losses.

Bathing and beach huts

Searching the surrounding areas, especially routes from the huts to the beach, can be rewarding and also check out sites of abandoned huts.

Beach steps

Search all around steps leading on to the beach and also underneath any wooden steps. Also look for signs of abandoned steps, which may hold older finds.

## Boat moorings

Searching at low tide, you will find many objects lost from the boats and the people on them.

## Caves and coves

Pirates and smugglers always needed somewhere to hide their loot and the nature of their activities often meant that many would have perished before reclaiming their booty. Thoroughly check caves out slowly and methodically, including floor, ceiling and walls. Take great care when exploring caves – always ensure you check the times of high and low tides and never go into a cave when the tide is coming in.

## Cliffs

Cliff faces are subject to constant erosion caused by sun, wind and tide. Centuries old treasures may be brought to the surface after a cliff fall. Some cliffs however, are prone to cliff falls so take heed of any warning notices and keep away. Accessible cliff paths are also worth searching.

## Dunes

Picnicking in sand dunes has been popular for centuries, so check any dunes and the paths leading to and from them, particularly after high winds which have caused sands to drift.

## Groynes

Sand and shingle moves along the beach, carrying lost metal objects with it, in the direction that the waves hit the beach by a process known as longshore drift. Wooden walls called groynes that extend from the beach into the sea are built to stop the beach washing away and you will see that the sand or shingle is built up higher on one side of the groyne, where material is deposited by wave action. Above high water people tend to use groynes as a windbreak or back rest. You will find coins and artefacts around groynes both above and below the high water mark.

## Paths

All accessible paths are worth searching and bear in mind dropped objects may also fall onto the verges of the path, so search these as well. If there are no obvious verges but open land at one or both sides of the path, then search the path and the open land out to at least the equivalent of the width of the path or in other words search an area at least three times the width of the path. The courses of paths often change over time so check old views and maps to see where the paths were.

## Piers

Over the years a great many coins and valuables have fallen through gaps between the wooden planks making up many walkways and will lie under and around the pier. The area around support legs often forms a natural trap owing to eddy currents. Many piers have been partially or totally lost to storms, fires and other causes, so check out the area where piers used to be, which you can find on old maps.

## Sea walls

The foot of seawalls and barriers act as collection points for objects thrown up by the tides and also, depending on the type of structure, for objects dropped from above by people walking and sitting. During storms, waves often crash over these defenses carrying metal objects with them, which you may find by checking the areas immediately above the sea walls.

## Super tips for beachcombers

Rock pools, high points and other areas where debris, driftwood, gravel, rubbish, seaweed, shells and small stones concentrate, are natural traps. These will also contain coins and other metal objects left behind by the receding tide. Check the rubbish carefully too – rings especially are often found trapped in seaweed.

Another type of trap found on some beaches are natural gullies running parallel with the tide line and, on the same beach, there may be several going all the way up the shore. These gullies may be a good many yards in length and vary in width from just a few inches to around a foot in width and depth. As the tides move over these gullies they act like riffles in gold panning, trapping heavy objects like coins and jewelery, being carried up and down the beach.

Bear in mind that the tides grade objects on sand and pebble beaches according to size and weight and you will often find coins of similar size in almost perfect rows. Larger coins and objects tend to be left higher up the beach than smaller.

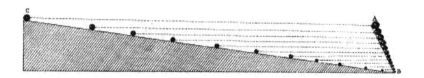

**Model showing grading of objects on a cross-section of beach**

A great time to hunt on a beach is immediately after a storm with an onshore wind and high seas. Onshore winds can strip beaches down to the hard pack or black sand, where the finds tend to settle naturally. Look out for a definite step formed in the beach around the high tide line – you will find metal objects dropped at the bottom of this step.

When metal detecting on a beach always be aware that you could find other, not necessarily metallic, objects such as wallets, purses, cameras, ship's cargo, relics, wooden chests, credit cards, paper money, books, handbags, binoculars, cell phones, etc. If you find anything that looks remotely dangerous – oil drums, weapons, ammunition, etc. – do not touch but mark the spot and tell the coastguard or police as soon as possible.

If you find anything valuable on a beach, other than loose change, where it may be possible to identify the owner, you are legally obliged to take reasonable steps to reunite the item with its owner. In the UK, in practice, it is probably easiest to report the find, at your earliest convenience, to the local police. You are not required to hand the item in to the police unless you wish to and in any case the item will be technically yours if not claimed within one calendar month. I say technically yours, as the owner may turn up at any time and claim rightful ownership, which is very unlikely to happen unless the find is extremely valuable. The police will return all unclaimed objects to the finder with the exception of cell phones, owing to the sensitive information they may contain. I have always found honesty to be the best policy and often you may be well rewarded, although the owner is under no obligation to give a reward and you must never ask for one. In Britain, if you find paper money on a beach which is unfit for circulation, the Bank of England will usually be able to replace it. Take any banknotes to your local bank in the first instance for advice.

The popular beach or resort of yesteryear is not necessarily popular today and it is a good idea to look in the local library, gift shops and book shops for any postcards, maps or local history books showing how the area looked in times gone by. Old photographs, postcards and maps can reveal the sites of vanished piers, moorings, buildings and beach huts. You could also speak to local people, especially the elderly, who may tell you about buried treasure, local legends, smugglers, lost ships and how things used to be. Most of this information will only be stories but you never can tell.

**Typical old seaside postcard**

Tidal rivers are an especially rich source of coins and artefacts. They are constantly being replenished not only by objects being washed downstream but also brought upstream by the tides from shipwrecks and other items lost at sea and on beaches. Learn as much as possible about the history of the river from the Internet or local library. Of particular interest are old bridges, moorings, buildings, warehouses, tow paths, boat houses, seamen's lodgings etc. Several tidal rivers also have or had ferry crossings and the hards or landing sites could make good search areas.

Ask local fishermen and boat owners about the history of the river – there may be tales of buried or sunken treasure and they will also tell you about the multitude of factors than can affect your decision as to where the best search sites might be.

Normally the best places to start searching a tidal river is not only on the river banks but around the 'high spots' that first appear when the tide recedes. As with beaches, these high spots could be real treasure troves. They act as obstructions as the water subsides and all types of debris, junk and rubbish accumulates around them. Amongst the rubbish you will also find what you are looking for.

## Case study: finding older losses

Sea charts lend themselves readily to beachcombers. Just as you can go and buy a land map, certainly in coastal parts, you can buy a sea chart. There are two series readily available in the UK – Admiralty Leisure and Imray Yachting Charts. Of the two I prefer the Imray version which shows drying features (the foreshore) pictorially rather than in abbreviated lettering. In the muddy parts hereabouts, I get more comfort in seeing a patch of stones depicted as dots rather than just the letters 'Sts'. You will have to pay about twice as much for a sea chart as for a land map; they say that a boat is a hole in the water into which you pour money and all associated services conspire to make that a self-evident truth. You can, of course, just stick with your land map, which will show one or two foreshore features such as stones and groynes but you may miss out on other important obstructions or finds traps like jetties, causeways and wrecks.

The area between high and low water is generally where not only jewlery is lost while swimming but also the older losses lie and what's more, the tides refresh the sites almost twice daily. The foot and mouth epidemic, in 2001, well and truly brought the potential of tidal foreshores home to me. On farmland I was finding Celtic, Roman, Saxon, Medieval and modern coins and artefacts, I was relegated to beaches and foreshores by the epidemic and with a little research into maps, charts and local histories, I was coming home with exactly the same range of objects, Celtic to modern. So, when all your productive fields are under crop or otherwise unavailable, don't be a stick-in-the-mud, do a little research on any beaches or tidal rivers you can get to and keep bringing home the finds.

Getting back to the foreshore, the first thing I like about stones, or Sts, is the safety factor, if stones don't sink then neither should you. Do be careful though as beaches and river foreshores can be dangerous. Always familiarise yourself with tide times and any local hazards; for example the tide in Morecambe Bay comes in as fast as a horse at the gallop. A few years ago 21 Chinese cockle pickers lost their lives because they were unaware of that fact! Walk out slowly and carefully, if you start to sink, back-up. Carry a whistle and don't venture out onto desolate foreshores without a suitable partner. The second thing I like about stones is that if the tides and currents drop stones, they'll also drop metal objects in the same place, so with safety and finds, it's a double whammy.

I must admit that I am fortunate in living on the coast and within easy reach of three tidal rivers with long histories. We tend to think of Dunwich in Suffolk, England, when we talk of submerged towns and villages but there is an awful lot more of them. I can name five near me without even trying. There is one that I have been maintaining a watching brief on for some time, which was also a borough and hence had a market. I have recovered a range of coins and objects from Iron Age to modern from there and recently found both an Edward the Confessor penny and a Cnut halfpenny in the same week. There is another large stony area on the same beach, where I found a silver ring – Celtic design but I think it's modern – an Edward VII shilling, and other pre-decimal coins. Another spot along the coast where the charts show ancient remains usually turns up something of interest. A friend found a Belgian medieval gold coin there and I have recovered a plain medieval ring brooch and a number of Georgian items including an 1811 one shilling and sixpence bank token. Another interesting find was part of a Victorian bracelet featuring a minstrel with a dog.

On the way to my metal detecting club meeting I have to pass a creek running off a tidal river which I thought I would take a look at. The town there is quite historically interesting having possessed a castle and medieval market. I arrived at low tide and looked at the creek first – although it looked stony and firm on the bottom where a trickle of water was running, there were mountains of mud to cross to get there and I thought NO, not on my own. However at the mouth of the creek there is a bit of a beach on the river so I thought I would give that a go. I had only seen the place at high tide before but at low tide it wasn't very picturesque unless you like car tyres, batteries, cans, bottles and bike frames. With some trepidation I went for it anyway. Well it was just nondescript bits of scrap for a while and then I found a coin – a George III halfpenny. So I concentrated searching around where I found the coin and found three £1 coins and then a Roman AE3 of Constantine with a good portrait. I found another two £1 coins and a few decimal coppers so it didn't turn out so badly after all.

Another area of beach I've started investigating which interests me is where they used to take horses and carts out to unload the ships and barges, so hopefully there should be old stuff out there. So far I found a lead bag seal marked 1777 (possibly Russian), quite a few decimal coins and the odd pre-decimal coin, including an Australian Edward VII six-pence and a Roman sestertius. I have to say the results have been very encouraging.

## Non-tidal water sites

As well as the sea, people have always been attracted to other areas of water – lakes, lochs, ponds, rivers and streams. Water courses have been used for centuries for bathing, fishing for food, industry, leisure, natural defence, pleasure, powering water mills, transport, washing clothes as well as a water supply for drinking and cooking. Since ancient times it has been customary to throw coins and other valuables into water, as a thank you for safe passage, an offering to the gods, to make a wish or just for the fun of it. Of necessity, farms and villages have been built around water courses for hundreds of years. Before the advent of swimming pools, thousands of people regularly relaxed by and swam in rivers and streams. Those days have gone but the coins and valuables they would have lost, still remain.

Before we talk about searching in water let's think about your safety – people sometimes drown in rivers. Avoid rivers in flood and be very careful when searching in water, especially fast flowing and deep water and particularly where the surface is swirling through eddies or currents. In the water, you should always check the bed in front of you with your detector, digger or scoop to ensure there are no deep holes. If possible take a friend with you or secure yourself, with a length of rope, to a fixed solid object on the bank. There is also the risk of contracting leptospirosis, commonly called Weil's disease, from rats' urine. The infection is commonly transmitted by allowing contaminated water to come in contact with unhealed breaks in the skin, or with the eyes, nose or mouth. Most cases occur in spring and autumn except in tropical areas, where it occurs all year-round. Flu-like symptoms with vomiting appear after a four to 14 day incubation period. Jaundice, red eyes, abdominal pain, diarrhea, and rash may also be experienced. I do not actually know of any metal detectorist contracting the disease but it is something to be aware of.

The best way to find objects on the bottom of rivers and streams is to work your way upstream so disturbed silt flows away from you. When you get a signal from your metal detector take a good scoop out the bed and tip it into a plastic sieve. Keep rechecking the hole with your detector and taking further scoops out of the bed into the sieve until you lose the signal, when the object will be in the sieve. You can make a floating sieve if you obtain a suitable sized car inner tube and lash the sieve into the centre of it. Don't forget to tie the sieve securely to yourself with a suitable length of strong line otherwise your sieve could go floating off and be lost.

Searching the banks and shallow water on either side of bridges would be a good place to start. Valuables have often been lost or thrown over the side of bridges especially by thieves needing to get rid of loot and weapons in a hurry. The bases of bridge supports act as traps for all manner of debris washed downstream but wherever you find such an accumulation, search thoroughly for coins and artefacts. Where a river or stream is deep or fast flowing, a bridge has probably been there for centuries but not necessarily in the same position. Many old bridges were built of wood and have been either replaced with stone or lost. The sites of old and demolished bridges make excellent metal detecting sites. Where rivers or streams are shallow or slow moving they would normally have been crossed on foot, horseback or carriage by means of a ford. Bridges have replaced most fords but the site of an old ford, which can often be identified by place names containing the word 'ford', is well worth searching.

Items lost beside bridges and fords can move hundreds of yards downstream before coming to rest perhaps in shallow water or near inner curves where the water is very deep and calm. Watch out for eddy currents swirling on the surface of the river, indicating an obstruction on the river bed, which can trap metal objects. Revisit productive areas at regularly intervals as they will be replenished as objects are continually washed downstream in a never ending process.

Also check tree roots encroaching into a river or stream as coins and valuables were often hidden in a bag or purse tied to the roots with cord and then submerged. Similarly, check tree branches for old ropes which may indicate the site of a swing.

Over the centuries several shelves can be created in rivers and streams as the water gradually erodes rock and earth. The corners of these shelves can contain a multitude of objects that have been left behind in times gone by. Along with searching the bed ensure you also search any shelves leading up the bank.

Bridge construction, dredging, droughts and floods are all opportunities for metal detecting. Coins and artefacts that have lain deeply buried for centuries can be brought into detection range. During severe drought certain water courses can dry up completely. Check these out as soon as possible as you may not get another chance for many years.

Dredging operations often result in material removed from the river bed being spread on nearby fields. Similarly, flooded rivers can overflow their banks and distribute their contents in adjacent fields. Rivers in flood can also permanently change course by forming a new cut and many water courses have been intentionally altered by man. Look for these alterations by comparing old and new maps. The former beds and banks could be very productive.

Check The Domesday Book and local histories for mills along water courses. These mill sites could have been used for centuries and are likely to be rich in old coins and artefacts. If the mill site is unknown just search along the original banks and you will very likely find hot spots where mills were operating.

Britain has over 2,000 miles of canals dating from the middle of the eighteenth century. The construction resulted in hundreds of houses being demolished and millions of tons of earth being excavated. Many thousands of labourers were employed who slept overnight in hastily erected camps and drank at the local taverns. You may find these sites through old maps and records. Other areas worth searching are all paths leading from the canals to towns or villages as well as lock gate areas, pub gardens, sites of demolished or abandoned buildings and tow paths.

While many waterways have been abandoned, dried up, fallen in to disrepair and perhaps filled in, many others are being strengthened and cleaned to keep them clear of debris, junk and weed and to ensure they remain navigable. Much cleaning and maintenance work is done voluntary, in the UK, by groups such as the Waterway Recovery Group, PO Box 114, Rickmansworth, WD3 1ZY. Tel: 01923 711114. Email: enquiries@wrg.org.uk. http://www.wrg.org.uk, who organise events throughout the main holiday periods, restoring derelict canals. Ask the project organiser if you can use your metal detector along the river or canal bank as well as on the silt and debris removed during cleaning. Always offer at least 50% of the proceeds of any finds towards project funds as money is always required for equipment and transport. See that you actually do the same amount of work as anyone else before using your detector and search at the end of the working day or during rest periods.

Do not forget the smaller water features like moats, ponds, springs, wells and the like; they are all sites with great potential. Ancient people were fascinated with springs particularly and would throw all manner of coins and artefacts into the water as offerings to their gods. Look out particularly for water containing an island, the ring of bright water so formed was fascinating to Celtic peoples and the area may be littered with gold coins.

## 5.2. Farmland and Other Inland Sites

Your own land in the UK, is the only place where you have a right to use a metal detector, and not even there, if your land happens to be defined as a Scheduled Ancient Monument or a Site of Special Scientific Interest. For most of us, our own land will consist of a garden or yard of some sort, which is nevertheless a very good place to start. Gardens will have seen much human activity in a relatively small area: gardening, sunbathing, alfresco meals, children playing, etc. Not to mention the possibility of metallic losses from whatever took place before the garden was laid out. I remember finding over 50 coins in my mother-in-laws 1920's garden and my most valuable single find, a Tudor iconographic gold ring, came from the garden of a 13th century house. So check out your garden and any other land you or your family owns or rents perhaps, although strictly you should obtain permission from the landowner if searching rented land as the landowner can claim any ownerless objects you may find. However if you are the occupier of the land as in the case of a garden or you have an allotment, for instance, the landowner is unlikely to object. You may only be looking for your own lost possessions there, after all.

Having searched your own land you will have a few finds to show and will undoubtedly be able to find relatives, friends, neighbours and work-mates willing to allow you to search their land also for a share in the finds. This simple approach of asking anyone and everyone you know could keep you busy with sites for quite some time.

Public parks, open spaces and other public areas are another possibility for searching. You can discover what parks and open spaces exist in your area, together with the contact details of the responsible local council department, from your local library or tourist information office. This information can be found online at:

http://local.direct.gov.uk/LDGRedirect/index.jsp?LGSL=461&LGIL=8

Bridleways, Footpaths and Public Rights of Way are usually owned by the landowner of the land, over which the path or way crosses. Where the way is fenced off from surrounding land the relevant highway authority – county or borough council, unitary authority or National Park authority often owns it and that would usually include roadside verges. The highway authority also has a statutory duty to keep all rights of way open and will certainly talk to the landowner if they receive complaints that your activities are in any way interfering with anyone's rights of free passage, so be careful!

In the early days of the hobby, in the UK, public areas were reckoned to be managed by custodians and reasonably accessible for metal detecting, as many still are in the USA. Following a British High Court ruling in the 1990's the local authority administering such areas was deemed to be the landowner and search permission needs to be obtained. A few enlightened councils do permit responsible metal detecting on public land and if your local council is among them, then find out what the rules are and you may have plenty of land to search.

If your local council bans metal detecting on their land, you may still be able to get permission but dealing with local government bureaucracy is fraught with difficulties and is not an experience for the faint hearted, so ensure, as best as you can, that the public places you want to search will be worth the effort. You will stand a much better chance of succeeding if you can claim most or all of the following:

*You are carrying out a specific project, preferably in a defined area.

*You live and presumably pay council tax in the council's area.

*You have NCMD or FID public liability insurance.

*You have knowledge and/or evidence of the council consenting to activities on amenity grassland which is more harmful than metal detecting – games, sports, funfairs, bonfires, horse-riding etc.

*You have knowledge and/or evidence of other members of the public taking issue with the council over activities in public open spaces.

You are unlikely to get a positive reply to your first letter. To win against officialdom you need to take the moral high-ground and keep responding with calm reasoned arguments and supporting evidence for your case. It might become a war of attrition but you stand a good chance of succeeding.

What are you paying your council tax for when they won't allow you to indulge in your harmless pastime? Why can anybody do almost anything else in the park without even asking? Why do they allow the funfair to drive huge trucks onto the park? Why do they allow the boy-scouts to have bonfires? If they say it's for charity, offer to give your decimal finds to charity. If they say they have a bylaw against metal detecting, ask for the documentation and the reason for the bylaw. The council can give exemptions from bylaws anyway – guide dogs for the blind are usually exempted from dog bylaws for instance.

If you are able to search on public land, leave your spade behind and only use small hand tools for finds extraction as a spade gives a very bad impression to the public who will undoubtedly be watching you. Also bear in mind that metal detectorists may have searched there before and most, if not all the easy targets, will already have been found. Your modern metal detector may go deeper than previous models used there but if you are not getting the finds, try the places which are more difficult to search, like under bushes.

Sooner or later you will undoubtedly graduate onto farmland. On farmland you seldom get the opportunity to completely cover anything other than the odd small area of arable land or larger areas under grass. Most fields used to be ploughed annually, ensuring a new crop of finds each year and land was left for relatively long periods before drilling, allowing searching for several months. Today, economic pressures on farming have reduced ploughing to a minimum, drilling of new seed taking place a few days after harvesting from the back of a cultivator. Now there's a new game afoot – direct drilling into stubble! The result is a much shorter detecting season on farmland. And if you detected from dawn to dusk you would be unlikely to thoroughly cover so much as an acre. So, unless your research or landscape observation has indicated certain areas will be more worthwhile than others, detecting tends to be very much a matter of sampling. A typical sampling method is shown in chapter 3.2. On ploughed fields, when you do find something of interest you should search a very large area around the location. Modern cultivation distributes soil, stones and other objects far and wide. Look carefully also for pieces of china, pottery, or oyster shells since any of these often have metal objects in amongst them.

Metal detector technology is constantly improving and objects not found some years ago could very easily be found today with a modern detector. Even if you or someone else has searched an area before, providing the site has potential, you should try again. Soil conditions are always changing and the last person who searched may have not been as thorough as you will be. No metal detectorist ever finds everything and you may have a better technique or a different detector to the one used by the searcher before you.

If you know how farming works you can maximise your searching of farmland and make finds throughout most of the year. The farmland of Britain is basically divided into about two-thirds grassland for animals and one-third arable land for crops. The west tends to be under grass and the east arable, with rainfall tending to be the defining factor. Always bear in mind that the farm produces the farmer's livelihood and do nothing that may interfere with that. Always come to an agreement (usually a 50/50 split and preferably in writing) about what is to happen to your finds and providing the item is not potential treasure, always give way if the farmer fancies a particular find, regardless of any agreement. The farmer may want you to call in each time you visit to check it is convenient for you to detect in a particular field and again when you have finished to show your finds, even if he says you can keep them all. Farmers are always busy, so don't outstay your welcome. As far as you are concerned, whatever the farmer says you can or cannot do on the farm, is law. Some farmers will be happy to let you detect on some crops, such as cereals, that are knee high, while others will want you off the field as soon as it is drilled. If you just accept and do what the farmer says, without argument, then you won't go far wrong and I'm sure it will not be long before you and your farmer become firm friends.

Lets take a look at arable land on which crops are regularly planted in the ground. There is a considerable variety of crops grown and I will only have room for generalisations here, so I advise you to do at least a little research on agriculture in your area. Most arable crops have both Winter (sown in the Autumn) and Spring sown varieties, while others, like root crops, are grown on a rotational basis for harvesting throughout the year. If a farmer is going to be sowing a spring crop, it is quite likely the field will be ploughed in the Autumn and left in this state until the Spring, for the frost to break down the soil, particularly on heavy or clay soils. In Spring there should be a couple of weeks after the crop has been drilled when the land will be flat and perfect for metal detecting. So, it is worth asking your farmer friends if they are leaving any land to over-winter for Spring sowing and asking them what crops are being sown and when.

Growing and climate conditions can make a difference of several weeks to the time crops are ready to harvest. Of the commonly grown grain and seed crops, Winter rape is usually harvested in late July or early August, followed by cereals, such as barley, oats and wheat and then peas and beans during August to September when maize and linseed are usually the last crops harvested. Once the crop has been harvested some sort of stubble will usually be left (pea stubble is almost none existent). Cereal crops tend to have very short stubble as the stalks are cut for straw for animal feed or perhaps fuel. The oilseeds and bean stalks are usually left around a foot (30cm) high, which makes detecting over them quite a challenge. If you are lucky the farmer may mow or disk them to make it easier for him to plough or cultivate the stubble back in to the ground. The problem with fresh stubble is it is difficult to push the detector search head through it and so you effectively lose detection depth. Maize is planted in rows around 30 inches (76cm) apart so you can detect in between the growing plants (with care) and the stubble after harvest. Stubble left for a few weeks soon starts to rot and softens up until it eventually becomes almost as easy as searching over grass.

Root crops like carrots, potatoes and turnips can be harvested throughout the year, while brassicas like, cabbage, cauliflower and sprouts can be harvested between July and October or even later. Some varieties of turnip are planted in Autumn to provide animal fodder in the ground over winter. The animals, particularly sheep, are fenced in to graze off the crop in strips leaving bare ground on which you can usually detect.

There have been subsidy schemes for farmers for a good number of years, which often result in many arable acres being left uncultivated for months or years. There is still a sort of 'set-aside' as it used to be called, where a field is left for the birds after harvest until the following Spring, when it will be sprayed off with a weedkiller and then cultivated and drilled with a new crop. Under the latest scheme in England, Countryside Stewardship, signed-up farmers will be leaving wide strips uncultivated around the edges of their arable fields, which might mean more detecting land.

Then there is fruit growing. Fruit trees such as apple, cherry and pear are usually planted in rows in orchards with a grass strip in between rows. Much soft fruit like blackcurrants, gooseberries and raspberries grow on bushes or canes and are usually laid out similarly to fruit trees, although the rows will be closer together. Apples and pears are usually picked or harvested in September or October, while soft fruits tend to be harvested throughout the Summer months. Once harvesting is finished, orchards should be available to search round to the following Spring when the blossom starts to appear, although there will be a short intermission during pruning. You can usually search both the bare earth around trees and bushes, (just be careful not to damage the roots on young stock) as well as the regularly mown grass strips. Once the blossom starts to appear it is probably a good idea to cease searching until after harvest so you avoid damaging the crop and also getting stung by bees, which are introduced into orchards to encourage pollination.

Grassland or pasture is very common in Britain and used basically for feeding farm animals. Some grass fields are grazed short by animals, while other fields are left to grow, animal free, and are mown a couple of times a year to produce hay or silage for feeding the animals during the winter months, when grass doesn't grow so well and the animals are often kept inside. Pasture offers plenty of opportunity for detecting in the winter months, when the grass is generally short and free of animals. Of course if the ground is frozen it will be difficult or impossible to dig finds out and on snow covered ground you will lose detection depth equivalent to the depth of snow. The only snow covered places possibly worth searching (for recent losses) are ski slopes and toboggan runs.

In warmer times of the year grassland for producing hay or silage will be searchable for a few weeks after mowing. Grazing land is searchable most of the year providing the farmer is happy to let you loose in amongst his animals. You also need to be comfortable detecting with grazing animals around you and to be very careful to fill your holes properly to avoid injured animals. If a horse or cow breaks a leg it usually has to be shot. Detecting with sheep is rarely a problem, they are timid creatures and tend to keep out of your way, unless they fancy that your finds bag contains food for them. Cows and calves tend to be inquisitive so you need to keep one eye on them while detecting; sometimes they'll completely ignore you and at other times the entire herd will come and see what you are up to. This can be a problem as they are large animals and unpredictably may jump around or even stampede, so if they get too close get out of their way or out of that particular field. And never ever detect in a field containing a bull. Horses are usually grazed alone or in small numbers in paddocks of just a few acres. Horses can kick and bite so you really need to know what the horse's temprament is before detecting with them. Likewise there are other creatures you may encounter, such as pigs, goats, llamas and rheas, which you'll need to take advice from the farmer before detecting among them.

There are two other issues with grassland that you need to be aware of. One is that in hot weather the ground can become very hard and dry. Finds become difficult to dig out and no matter how careful you reinstate the ground, the grass will die off leaving unsightly patches where you have been digging, holes can even reform if the dead grass gets kicked out by animals. You can mitigate this by dragging a considerable quantity of water around with you and watering the grass, you have removed, back into the ground but is it worth the effort? The other issue is that on permanent grassland you will be up against the law of diminishing returns on the finds you make, since metal objects sink and other than the action of burrowing animals, there is nothing to bring them back up into the surface layers. Once a pasture field stops producing, the only way you will get more finds out of it is to search with a deeper-seeking metal detector.

Forest and woodland makes up about 10% of the land in Great Britain and has considerable potential for metal detecting for much ancient woodland has seen activity for centuries in harvesting wood for building, charcoal, fencing and kindle; grazing pigs; hiding of valuables and shelter for fugitives, robbers and smugglers. Quite often sites of early industry and substantial former homes will be hidden in woodland and well worth searching. The Forestry Commision manages some 700,000 hectares (1.7M acres) of land in England and Scotland, unfortunately they only allow metal detecting on archaeological projects. Nevertheless there are many parcels of woodland in private ownership where metal detecting permission could be obtained.

Woodland is generally available for searching all year round, offering some protection from high winds, rain and snow. And in freezing conditions, woodland floors rarely become frozen solid. The major drawback in deciduous and mixed woodland is the build up of decayed leaves, which deeply covers older losses and the soil acidity around conifers rapidly corrodes most buried metals. In summer thick undergrowth can inhibit searching and you will need a copious supply of insect repellent to avoid being eaten alive.

Whatever type of land you choose to search and really you should endeavour to build a portfolio of different types that will potentially allow you to metal detect throughout the year. However, all land is not equal for if you habitually search land where nothing much happened in the past then your finds bag will contain nothing much. The following chapter details specific research you can carry out to improve your finds and interest, however there are a number of landscape features you can search on or around, which will generally hold more losses than surounding featureless areas. The list is not exhaustive by any means but should give you a taste of what to look for:

*Allotments

*Battle sites. Most known sites of the actual battle will be protected but surrounding areas, where the armies camped may not be. Also military muster sites.

*Beauty spots, mount pleasants, picnic areas, south facing slopes.

*Buildings of any sort such as barns, bridges, churches, dwellings, garages, industrial, inns, mills, railway lines (disused), roads, schools, towers.

*Butts where archery was practised.

*Campsites; tent or caravan; holiday, military, scouts and guides.

*Car boot sites.

*Carparks (not hard-surfaced except for eyes-only finds).

*Circus and carnival sites.

*Concerts and festivals, bandstands.

*Crowd attractions: boxing, cock fights, executions, wrestling.

*Earthworks such as banks and ditches (check they are not scheduled ancient monuments).

*Fair and fairground sites.

*Market sites.

*Paths and trackways.

*Parks, games pitches, lidos, playgrounds.

*Races; car, horse, running.

*Routes of marches and rallies, marching armies.

*Trees, especially large and old trees and hedges or former hedge lines. A rough guide to estimating the age of a hedge is to count the number of different species and multiply by 25 years.

*Water or former water features such as ditches, lakes, moats, ponds, rivers, streams, wells.

# 6. Research

It was one of those detecting club meetings when the thorny subject of having no 'decent' land to detect on raised, its ugly head yet again. "Look!" I said. "All you have to do is carry out a little easy site research and communicate the results to the landowner. It makes gaining detecting permission much easier and you'll make more and better finds. What's more your hobby will be more interesting, as you will know why the finds are there."

"It's okay for you." Somebody responded. "You have access to hundreds of acres of productive farmland and you are positively tripping over good finds." "Yes that's true." I said. "But I only got that through site research. Why don't you just do the same?"

"We don't know how to do it!" Came the chorus. Thirty highly intelligent, highly experienced, highly motivated detectorists and between them they didn't have a clue about where to begin!

I was stunned. I had started in the early years of the metal detecting hobby when the much-quoted maxim was 'research really pays', and had taken that to heart to the extent that I rarely switched on my detector on a new site, unless I had done some research first. But thinking about it, even though librarians are among the most helpful people on the Planet, you can't go into a library and ask the librarian to find you a productive detecting site. They just wouldn't know what to look for. But since I do, I'll give you my top research tips:

* Start your research near home or in a place, where you are already known. You will have less travelling to do (so more detecting time) and you will find it easier to get permission.

* Visit your local public library; it will have a local history section containing relevant books and maps. Once you have exhausted its resources or you need something that isn't held there, the librarian will be able to advise you of other libraries and archives where you can obtain more research material. Libraries also have computers for public use these days, so if you don't have your own computer, the library is the place to go.

* The Internet is the biggest library on the Planet so if you have access to a computer you can do a considerable amount of research without leaving home and when the library is closed. The most popular search engine is Google and you can get a lot of information just by entering the name of the place you are interested in along with the word: history, ancient, old, Roman, etc.

* Archaeology UK's database of Archaeological sites (ARCHI, http://www.digital-documents.co.uk) is a fully searchable database of the locations of more than 165,000 archaeological sites, which range from single coins and artefacts to standing buildings. See what has been found in your area

of interest and you can almost guarantee finding more of the same. You would need to subscribe to get the best out of ARCHI, nevertheless, the free search facility is well worthwhile.

* The earliest usable maps of a reasonable scale are likely to be county maps. Get hold of the earliest map you can find for your county and make a note of all features within your chosen area. Everything on the map will be at least as old as the map (probably considerably older) and important too. You will find abbeys, bridges, castles, churches, ferries, manors, parks, ports, priories, etc. If the feature still exists, you may not be able to search it but any surrounding land will hold losses dating at least as old as the feature. True Treasure Books (http://www.truetreasurebooks.net/products-page/map) stock superbly reproduced Victorian maps for every UK county.

* Large scale tithe maps, drawn mainly between 1836 and 1841, covering roughly 80% of England and Wales have sometimes been called the detectorist's map as, together with the accompanying award or apportionment, they show and name every field and plot of land, together with boundaries, owners and land use throughout entire parishes.

* Other maps you will find invaluable are Ordnance Survey maps one inch to one mile (1801- 1971); Landranger 1.25 inch to one mile from 1971; 2.5 inch to one mile from 1935 becoming the Pathfinder (which I prefer for its greater coverage of archaeological find spots) and then the Explorer. After 1850 large scale six inch and twenty-five inch to one mile maps were introduced, defining the landscape accurately and in minute detail.

* Ordnance Survey have also produced a number of useful historical maps including Ancient Britain, Britain in the Dark Ages and Roman Britain.

* The urban detectorist would do well to look out for Ordnance Survey town plans produced from the 1840s for many towns and cities at scales between 5 feet and 10.56 feet to one mile.

* All schemes for canal, road and railway construction as well as river alterations had to have an Act of Parliament and, from 1792, an exact plan, which has resulted in some of the earliest large-scale maps for many places.

* Look out for estate maps dating before 1850 in your County Archives. These early detailed maps, some going back to Tudor times, could be your passport to a new farm and exciting finds.

* Sea charts are not just for beachcombers, they also map coastal inland sites on a large scale that pre-dates Ordnance Survey.

* When all your productive fields are under crop or otherwise unavailable, research any beaches or tidal rivers you can get to and keep bringing home the finds.

* Since around the year 2000, Britain has been extensively photographed from the air to produce seamless photographic maps, which are available on the Internet at Google Earth (http://engall.filewin.com/Google-Earth/?p=UK-ADC-en). CDROMs and printed maps and atlases are also available. There is fantastic scope for locating sites by studying these maps as you gain an overview by locating ancient banks, ditches, fortifications, settlements, tracks and watercourses which may only be visible as crop marks from the air.

* A good place to start your research is to consult an early relevant county history, which will give you an eye witness account of your county at the time with particular interest in the wealthies and worthies who had money and other valuables to lose. Good starting volumes for the UK would be: The Beauties of England and Wales, The Victoria County History, The County Histories of Scotland, Ordnance Survey Memoirs of Ireland

* **The Domesday Book** of 1086 records a fascinating snapshot of eleventh century life in all but five English counties. Every site mentioned such as manors, churches, villages, mills, markets, etc. must be over 900 years old and, with the land surrounding them, will make fantastic metal detecting sites.

**Researching farm history**

To give you an example of how to carry out research, here is a report on one of my own projects.

When I was offered the chance to search a farm in the neighbouring county of Sussex, I heeded my own words and knuckled down to some serious research. I have shelves full of books and draws full of maps covering my home county of Kent but on foreign soil, as it were, I had little information. Where do you start? Start at the present time with what is already known or rumoured.

The farm manager told me the farmhouse was a former manor house dating back to the 13th century; there was a 16th century oast house and ancient watermill adjacent to the land, which was crossed by the pilgrims' way. All interesting stuff but it is wise to verify what you are told, while not arguing with your source, of course.

Apparently the previous landowner greeted visitors with the barrel of a shotgun, so not much historical investigation of the farm had taken place until fairly recently. The current landowner, however, had commissioned an archaeological survey of the house, which dated it back to at least the 15th century, so that was a good start. Looking at the Guide to County Histories in my book, **Site Research**, I realized I had a copy of the early 19th century series: **The Beauties of England and Wales**, covering Sussex but was disappointed to read that the compilers of the history for the two most relevant parishes had failed to meet the publication deadline! You win some, you lose some!

Another tome I have on my shelves is the complete **Domesday Book** covering the entire survey of 34 English Counties. Parish boundaries had changed in this area over time, effectively moving the farm from a declining old parish to an expanding new one. There is no mention of the newer parish in the Domesday Book but the old parish was actually recorded as a hundred in 1086 and possessed one (water) mill. The Domesday water mill may be the one still standing next door to the farm and clearly there must be a hundred meeting site around somewhere, in fact there is a Hundred House within the parish which is said to be the meeting place.

Turning to the site guide in **Successful Detecting Sites** I was pleased to discover that the three nearest settlements; north east and west of the farm, which I located on the county map printed in the book, had all held fairs in the past, so there was a good chance that fairgoers had been crossing the farm for several hundred years, sprinkling it with losses.

With my personal resources exhausted, nearer home I could have popped down to the local library or county archives but here would need a full day out to make it worthwhile. Before making that trip, I decided to see what I could find out on the Internet. If you want to try such research but you are not a computer user, you can easily become one down at your local library.

ARCHI, an acronym derived from archaeological index, is a good place to start. The site index on Archaeology UK http://www.archiuk.com/ lists over 165,000 UK sites ranging from single coin finds to major ancient monuments, its great value from my point of view is that most entries have been gleaned from sources outside metal detecting, so you probably will not find other detectorists already on your chosen site. To perform a basic search you simply enter the relevant postcode or place and select 3km, 5km or 10km distance, click 'begin search' and ARCHI will return all finds within the distance specified. If you are not a subscriber you will get a description of the find and a distance from the postcode, while subscribers will also get direction, findspot and access to modern map, old map and aerial photograph. If you use ARCHI frequently, then the few pounds asked for an annual subscription is time saving and good value for money. A 3km search returned over forty sites, ranging from a Celtic gold coin find to a deserted medieval village, so there was plenty of history in the area. As a subscriber I had instant access to the findspots otherwise I would have had to Google the site details and hope for the best.

Another on line index or database well worth consulting is the Historic Environment Record (HER): http://www.heritagegateway.org.uk/gateway/chr/ this is the former Sites and Monuments Record (SMR) and tends to concentrate on larger sites than ARCHI such as buildings and earthworks. In some counties Portable Antiquities Scheme (PAS) data for single finds may be included but only to a four figure grid reference. What the HER search did turn up for the parish was a track way of probable prehistoric or Roman date, which ties in nicely with the Roman furnace.

The **Ordnance Survey map of Roman Britain** did not show this track way, however the foremost authority on Roman roads in Britain was the late Ivan D Margary whose major work was two volumes of **Roman Roads of Britain** published in the 1950s. I did have one of Margary's other works, **Roman Ways of the Weald**, which covered this particular track way running very near or perhaps even through the farm.

An excellent way of finding historical information on the Internet is simply to type into a search engine the name of the county/parish/town/village followed by 'history' and see what turns up. Sussex top spot on Google was 'Sussex History – A Free online history library' with some useful old publications included but a similar search on the parish name produced much better results. The top position was 'The Weald of Kent, Surrey and Sussex', which held a vast database of historical information: books, documents, photographs and, very importantly, maps. In fact there was a range of downloadable maps from John Speed, 1610 to Ordnance Survey, 6 inch to 1 mile, 1899.

Although the relevant pages of the listed sources had been digitised and could be accessed from the site, in some cases the information was incomplete so I thought it would be a good idea to try and obtain more complete sources. A vast number of old publications have been made available for free reading and free download in the last few years. Two sites I find invaluable for gaining access to this mine of information are: Google Books http://books.google.com/ and Internet Archive: http://archive.org/ I use the two because what I can't find on one site I can often find on the other. I managed to find and download both volumes of: **A Compendious History of Sussex** by Mark Antony Lower (1870), which not only gave a good historical description of parishes I was interested in but also indexed the first twenty volumes of the **Sussex Archaeological Collections**, the journal of the Sussex Archaeological Society formed in 1848. Many of these old journals were also available for reading and download on the two sites, so I was able to follow up some of the references.

Another invaluable resource from Google is Google Earth: http://engall.filewin.com/Google-Earth/?p=UK-ADC-en free software showing aerial views of the entire planet. The major benefit of looking at aerial photographs is that they may show crop marks caused by buried features producing differential growing rates. Crop mark hunting has been made even easier on Google Earth now as you can turn back the clock and view a number of different surveys made during the last dozen years or so. To use the feature, click on the clock icon on the tool bar to reveal the time slider. Although Google Earth allows you to print the aerial photo it doesn't provide much in the way of editing facilities and you can end up with quite a small print. To get around this you can hit the 'Print Screen' button on your keyboard, which copies the current screen onto the clipboard, then paste into MS Paint or a photo editor where you can edit the picture and print from there.

The tithe or enclosure map really is a must for farm history research as it documents every single field and plot of land in many parishes at a very large scale. Tithe maps came about from The Tithe Commutation Act of 1836, whereby the Church's 10% tax on annual produce from the land was commuted from goods to cash, necessitating a very detailed record of the land and its use. The parish I was looking at was covered by a tithe map; however some parishes never had such a map, often this is because their tithes had already been commuted by an earlier enclosure act, in which case the enclosure award and map could just as usefully be studied.

Fields and plots of land on both tithe maps and enclosure maps are numbered and refer to the separate apportionment in the case of tithe maps and award in the case of enclosure maps. Unfortunately only a few tithe or enclosure maps are available online at present so for most places a visit to the local library, county archives or The National Archives is probably the way to go. However, The British Library has a useful county guide to online and digitised tithe maps here: http://www.bl.uk/reshelp/findhelprestype/maps/tithemaps/tithemaps.html from where I discovered that Sussex had put its tithe maps on CD, which could be viewed at certain libraries or purchased for a few pounds for use on a PC at home. Some apportionments, which are absolutely essential for interpreting the map, were also available on CD or by email. Where you can only get the tithe maps alone, you can buy the relevant apportionment from the sales page at ARCHI: http://www.digital-documents.co.uk/archi/tithlist.htm or by clicking on Field Name Lists on the menu at the top of the page.

Having tracked down the tithe or enclosure map and corresponding apportionment or award, what use can you make of them? There are several great uses:

Once enclosure got under way, fields were named so illiterate agricultural workers in the past could easily navigate the landscape at their master's bidding, without the need of maps or complex instructions. The field names often refer to vanished buildings or routes, meeting or trading places, sporting events and other activities that were guaranteed to put metallic losses in the ground. So by studying these field names, productive sites will be found. The names of trading and meeting sites are discussed in **Successful Detecting Sites** and others will be found analysed in the relevant county volumes published by The English Place-Name Society.

If you have picked up a lead from elsewhere describing a feature, event or find in a particular named field and need to find the actual field, the map will probably reveal all.

The state of cultivation of fields recorded in the apportionment can guide you to the probable site of an event. A fair that was held at the time of the survey, for instance, would most likely take place on grassland rather than an arable field.

The map itself shows field boundaries, buildings, tracks and footpaths as they were nearly 200 years ago, which you can compare to a modern map and highlight the changes.

I have ordered the tithe map and apportionment, covering the farm, to be delivered, rather than spend valuable detecting time and money visiting the archives, so while I am waiting, I've started detecting. Based on what I have discovered so far the hot spots are likely to be all searchable land around the main house, all routes across the site and the frontage along the river.

In summary: research, research, research! If you habitually go metal detecting where nothing much happened in the past then all you are likely to find is – nothing much. You need to concentrate on searching sites where there was human activity in the past and the more numerous and wealthy the humans the more you are likely to find with your metal detector. You can start by visiting your local library and reading about the local history of your neighbourhood.

# 7. Identification of Finds

Scrap metal will undoubtedly be your most common find but it is all worth some money these days, so don't throw it in the hedge or put it back in the ground, where you might end up digging it up again. Take it home and segregate it into finds, unidentified finds (you may find something really interesting or valuable in that lot later) and scrap: gold, silver, copper-alloys, lead, aluminum, iron and the rest. When you have saved a worthwhile amount, sell it to a scrap metal merchant.

## Identification of metals

After carefully washing your find the next step is to try and determine of what metal it is made.

Aluminium: a soft, light, white metal not produced commercially until 1854 so finds won't be very old. May be shiny or have a grey tarnish or white corrosion.

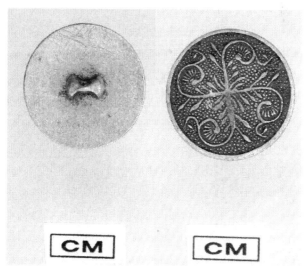

**Aluminium button**

Copper and alloys: copper and bronze (copper-tin alloy) are a red-brown colour; brass (copper-zinc alloy) is yellow; cupronickel (copper-nickel alloy) and nickel silver (copper-zinc-nickel alloy) are both silver or white coloured. Excavated copper-alloys are usually either smooth green or black (may be patchy with bare metal) or powdery green.

83

**Copper-alloy coins**

Gold: a soft, heavy, yellow metal, which usually comes out of the ground bright and shiny. Gold alloys may show green (copper) or purple (silver) spots or hue. In modern jewellery gold is often specially alloyed to produce other colours such as white or rose (red).

**9 carat gold signet ring**

Iron and steel: a grey, magnetic metal that is usually found covered in lumpy orange rust (except stainless steel, which usually remains bright and shiny). Test with a magnet, if the magnet sticks the metal is (or contains) iron or steel.

84

**10 ounce iron cannon ball**

<u>Lead:</u> a soft, heavy, grey metal often excavated with a white or grey surface coating. Lead is a poison, which can be absorbed through human skin so handle with waterproof gloves.

**Engraved lead object**

Nickel: a hard silvery-white metal discovered in 1751. Pure nickel is used for specialist tools and equipment such as medical and laboratory ware, otherwise it is usually found alloyed with copper and other metals as either a modern coining metal or tableware. Cupro-nickel coins often have a red colour as a result of the copper leaching out.

**Cupro-nickel coin**

Pewter: a white to grey alloy of lead and tin. Excavated pewter is usually dark grey, may be flaky and may have a white to grey surface coating.

**Pewter spoon handle**

Platinum: a white, heavy shiny metal mostly used in fairly modern jewellery (discovered 1735).

Silver: a white metal, which may come out of the ground bright and shiny or have a smooth black tarnish or white, grey, lilac or green (when alloyed with

86

copper) corrosion. May be very brittle and easily cracked. Oils and salts in the skin attack silver so it is best handled wearing cotton or waterproof gloves.

**Silver Victoria shilling, silver medallion, silver medieval coin**

Tin: a white metal, which usually has a dull earthy surface when excavated, usually found as a protective coating on iron or steel.

**Charles II tin farthing**

Zinc: a dull grey metal usually excavated as bare metal but may have white powdery spots, often in deep pits. Although used by the Romans, alloyed with copper for coinage, Zinc finds will be relatively modern.

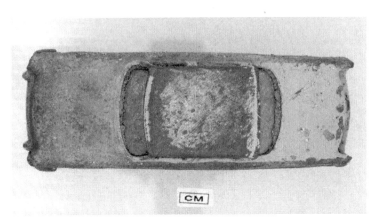

**Die-cast zinc model car. (roof stripped of paint to show bare metal)**

There are also a few unusual metals such as <u>Titanium</u> and <u>Palladium</u> that are mainly used in modern jewellery, so if you find anything that doesn't fit into the above I'm afraid you'll have to seek out specialist advice. If the object is jewellery then your local independent jeweller will probably be able to help.

**Palladium finger ring**

## A Brief History of Metal Finds

Metal artefacts first appeared in the Bronze Age and have expanded in type and variety ever since. Typical dates and divisions of the periods are given below but bear in mind that the dates are generally aproximations and there was a gradual change from one period to the next. The issue is also somewhat confused by the use of different date ranges and alternative names. I am using the British Museum version for the main divisions, underlined, but have given common alternative names and date ranges in brackets.

Bronze Age (Prehistoric): C. 2500 – 700 BC

Early: C. 2500 – 1500 BC; Middle: C. 1500 – 1150 BC; Late: C. 1150 – 700 BC

Metal finds of the Bronze Age will usually be copper-alloy (bronze) tools or weapons. There is also the possibility of gold jewelry in the form of torcs (twisted wire neck and arm rings) and high status gold vessels like the Ringlemere cup.

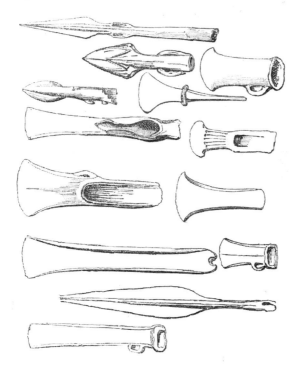

**Bronze Age tools and weapons**

Iron Age (Prehistoric, Celtic): C. 700 BC – 43 AD

Early: C. 700 – 350 BC; Middle: C. 350 – 100 BC; Late: C. 100 BC – 43 AD

Tools and weapons were generally made of iron but will not often be found owing to corrosion and metal detector discrimination settings. More often found will be fittings in bronze, such as knife handles and sword and dagger pommels.

Clothing fasteners in the form of brooches and toggles started to be used. Iron Age bow brooches were made of copper-alloy, which, in their simplest form, looked similar to a modern day safety pin, although there were annular brooches and the more ornamental dragonesque brooches. Copper-alloy pendants also appeared and high status adornment continued in the form of gold torcs and finger rings.

Copper-alloy mounts for attachment to leatherwork belts and buckets were used together with fittings associated with horses, such as strap junctions and terret rings. A unique cosmetic implement in the form of a woad grinder was introduced and hand-held mirrors are also occasionally found.

**Iron Age strap junction**

Although there is a school of thought that bronze axe heads were used as a type of early currency, iron bars and gold ring money was used in the Iron Age, developing into a coin based currency from the Middle Iron Age, with the introduction of a range of copper-alloy, silver and gold coins.

**Iron Age potin coin, c. 50BC**

Roman 43 – 410 AD

(Romano-British C. 100 BC – 100 AD)

The list of artefacts left in the soil by the Romans is quite enormous compared to previous ages and the range and variety expanded accordingly.

Tools and weapons generally continued to be made of iron, often with fittings in copper-alloy, such as knife handles and sword and dagger pommels. Iron horseshoes in the form of strap on hippo-sandals also appear.

Brooches developed into a great variety of more elaborate affairs, with flat plate and zoomorphic brooches coming into use. Most Roman brooches are made of copper-alloy, often with coloured enamelling. Pendants, many of an erotic nature, also continued, which were made mainly in copper-alloy and occasionally silver or gold. Dress pins became fairly common.

Copper-alloy mounts for attachment to leatherwork, utensils and furniture were used, while figurines and small statues are sometimes found. Spoons made from copper-alloy or silver are occasionally found along with other domestic ware such as pans and plates (pateras). Finger rings are quite common in copper-alloy, silver and gold. Buckles, seal boxes and keys appeared as did steelyards and associated weights.

**Roman furniture mount featuring Bacchus**

91

Copper-alloy clapper bells, which are more or less conical, open at the widest end and fitted with a swinging arm or clapper, appear in Roman times. Cosmetic or medical implements such as ear scoops and dental picks in copper-alloy or silver are also found.

The Romans had a well developed coin based currency system, which changed frequently with the emperors, producing a huge range of copper-alloy, silver and gold coins.

**Roman bronze coin of Fausta, 307-337**

Early Medieval (Saxon)

Early (Dark Ages): C. 410 – 720 AD; Middle (Dark Ages): C. 720 – 850 AD; Late (Viking): C. 850 – 1066 AD (Anglo-Norman: C. 1000 – 1100 AD)

Coins (mainly silver) and artefacts are quite scarce finds from this period and often the artefacts are of high quality and may be gilded or even solid silver or gold. Weapons and shield bosses are often associated with a male burial, whereas personal adornments may indicate a female burial.

Tools and weapons generally continued to be made of iron, often with fittings in copper-alloy, such as knife handles and sword and dagger pommels. Iron shield bosses are occasionally found. Horseshoes, made of iron, take on the modern form but generally have a wavy edge. Horse harness fittings are found in the form of strap fittings and bridle cheek pieces as well as stirrup mounts. Belt and scabbard fittings include buckles, chapes, mounts and strap ends.

In the Early Medieval period bow brooches became even more elaborate; plate brooches developed into button and saucer brooches and annular (solid ring) or penannular (open ring) brooches appeared. Again many brooches are copper-alloy but usually gilded and may feature enamel or stones such as garnets. High status brooches in silver or gold can also be found. Dress pins are also found. There were a large variety of pendants in use in bronze, silver and gold. Finger rings are occasionally found typically made from silver or gold twisted wire. Hooked clothing fasteners, keys and tweezers also turn up.

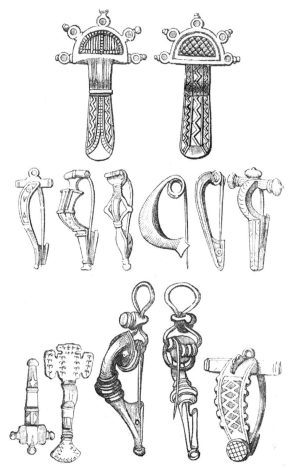

**Early Medieval Brooches**

## Medieval C.1066 – 1500 AD

Tools and weapons generally continued to be made of iron, often with fittings in copper-alloy, such as knife handles and sword and dagger pommels. Horseshoes, made of iron, take on the modern form but generally are keyhole shaped. Horse harness fittings are generally confined to pendants, often heraldic, with enamel. Belt and scabbard fittings include buckles, chapes, mounts and strap ends.

Medieval brooches are usually annular, typically in copper-alloy but considerable numbers of silver and even gold versions are found. Pins in copper-alloy and silver are also found. Finger rings become more common.

93

The crotal or rumbler bell, which is usually spherical (sometimes pear shaped), enclosing a loose iron ball or pea to generate sound and having a suspension loop for attachment to (usually) animals, came in to regular use. These were mainly made in copper-alloy, tin or pewter and date to 13th – 15th centuries but may be as late as 19th century.

Lead seals and seal matrices in lead, copper-alloy and occasionally silver are fairly regular finds from this period. As well as personal seal matrices there are large circular lead seals, called Papal Bullae, originally attached to documents from the Vatican. Cloth, bag and sack seals in lead can also be found. Pilgrimmages were popular during this period and there are lead ampullae (for holy water) and pilgrims' badges found.

Many of the artefacts that we are familiar with today came into regular use during this period:

* Buttons appeared in the 14th century and are cast in one-piece from copper-alloy or pewter.

* Change purses were made of leather or cloth but were suspended from a copper-alloy purse bar.

* Keys, many made of copper-alloy are found quite regularly.

* Thimbles of copper-alloy, having a closed top, date from 1350.

* Weights for trade of copper-alloy and lead; coin weights of copper-alloy and lead loom weights and spindle whorls used for spinning and weaving.

232 and 233. Pence of William I. or II.  235. Angel of Henry VI.  237. Quarter-noble of Henry IV.
234. Penny of Edward I.  236. Shilling of Henry VII.  238. Gold penny of Henry III.

**Medieval coins**

94

The basic coin was the silver penny or sterling, which was divided into halfpennies and farthings by cutting the penny into fractions. From the 12th century round halfpennies were produced, followed by round farthings from the 13th century. The silver penny remained as the highest denomination until the silver groat of fourpence was coined from 1279 and halfgroat added in 1351. The silver coinage continued unaltered in range from farthing to groat until the last years of the medieval period when Henry VII added the testoon or shilling of twelve pence. Gold coinage in the form of the Noble (80 pennies), half-noble and quarter-noble was struck from 1344. In 1464 the Ryal or rose-noble of ten shillings, was introduced, with halves and quarters, and the noble was effectively renamed the Angel. Half-angels were struck from 1470. A sovereign of 20 shillings was added in 1485.

There was no official base metal coinage in England during this period. Copper-alloy jettons were introduced for accounting and may have been used as small change however.

Post Medieval C.1500 – 1800 AD

(Tudor: C.1500 – 1600 AD); (Stuart: C.1600 – 1700 AD); (Georgian (Hanoverian): 1715 – 1837)

As we head into the age of industry and invention there is a proliferation of both coinage and metal artefacts. A few highlights are:

* The table fork comes into use.

* Posy (the forerunner of wedding and engagement rings) and memorial or mourning rings in gold (mainly) and silver become popular.

* Firearms come into use with lead amunition (musket and pistol balls). Toy pistols and canons are also found.

* Tobacco for smoking and snuff is imported from the colonies (America). Pipe tampers and other tools become popular.

* Thimbles with open tops, called sewing rings, appear.

* Fittings (mainly copper-alloy) on furniture become common

* Post Medieval and Modern brooches tend to be much more ornate and come in a great variety of forms. Many will be silvered or gilded copper-alloy but there is an increased chance of finding solid gold and silver examples.

The method of coin production changes from hammered to milled (using a coin press). The increasing price of silver reduces the penny to a very small size and copper farthings and halfpennies replace the silver penny for small change. Shortage of small change generates periods of unofficial token production in lead (16th-17th centuries) and copper-alloy (17th and 18th centuries).

**A range of Post Medieval and Modern finds**

Modern 1800 AD – present

(Victorian 1837 – 1901)

Modern finds are much more common than finds from earlier periods principally because there were more people around who had metal objects to lose. Most modern metal objects are machine made and this shows up in the regular shape and design. Screw threads are largely a modern invention so if your artifact has a screw thread it will almost certainly be modern. Most horse furniture (brasses etc.) dates from Victorian to early 20th century. Railways came into being in the 1820s and the motor car in the 1890s so anything related to either can only be modern.

After a brief show of tokens in the early 19th century, there was a re-coinage resulting in coins being very much as they are today. However, during the 20th century gold and silver ceased to be used for coins in normal circulation to generally be replaced by nickel-brass and cupro-nickel. As a result of rising metal prices, lower value coins are increasingly being made from plated steel.

## Identification Resources

Coins are fairly easy to identify and value from catalogues, even an old catalogue is useful and will give a relative value. **Coins of England & the United Kingdom**, (Spink, published annually), is the main British catalogue.

There are World Coin Catalogues and catalogues covering many foreign countries providing you can identify which country issued the coin in the first place.

I only know one general catalogue of artefacts which is **Benet's Artefacts of England & the United Kingdom**, (Greenlight Publishing, 2003), this is beautifully illustrated with colour photographs of high quality artefacts. If your find is in Benet's then you will know you have arrived! You will also know the value and can proceed accordingly. Greenlight Publishing: http://www.greenlightpublishing.com/PBCPPlayer.asp?ID=1143155 produce a wide range of books on identifying finds, many with valuations. Many detectorists build their own library of reference books for identification but if you are just starting out you could try the public library.

Your Finds Liason Officer or local museum curator can usually assist in finds identification and relative scarcity rather than valuation but they won't be expert in all types of metal object, although they can usually find a specialist in whatever you show them. Most FLOs hold finds identification days. Metal detecting magazines, such as **The Searcher**, usually have finds identification and valuation services.

The Portable Antiquities Scheme (PAS) http://www.finds.org.uk has a large database of finds with nearly a million objects recorded at time of writing; which will help with identification although not valuation. There is a facility however to search the Treasure Annual Reports, which record values where the objects have been declared treasure and the treasure annual reports themselves can be downloaded as a pdf file (Adobe Acrobat) from: http://www.finds.org.uk/treasure You will find the reports on the left sidebar. Record your own finds with the PAS too, providing you have the landowners permission, as that will help all of us and gives something back for what we are taking away.

The UK Detector Finds Database can be searched at http://www.ukdfd.co.uk although again there are no valuations. UK Detector Net http://www.forumukdetectornet.co.uk hosts the largest British metal detecting forum on the internet, which also has a finds identifying section and you should be able to obtain a valuation too.

Many small metal objects are offered for sale on Ebay http://www.ebay.co.uk or http://www.ebay.com so you can search completed listings to see what prices were achieved and if you know what an object basically is you can search for information in a search engine such as Google http://www.google.co.uk or http://www.google.com

# 8. Cleaning and Conservation

Look after your finds. You've worked hard to recover your finds, the last thing you want to do is to throw them in a box and leave them to corrode to dust, for if you don't take a few basic precautions that is what is likely to happen. A useful FREE guide to conservation is available from the Portable Antiquities Scheme (PAS) http://www.finds.org.uk/conservation/ or your local Finds Liaison Officer.

Once you remove a metal find from the ground, on one hand you save that object from the ravages of agricultural machinery, fertilisers or the sea but on the other hand you trigger decay in most metals that could lead to total destruction unless you take steps to preserve your find.

There are two agents necessary for the corrosion of metals to take place – moisture and oxygen. If we can eliminate one or the other then we can effectively stop any further corrosion taking place. I remember a school science experiment demonstrating that iron nails will not rust if kept under water, which had been previously boiled to remove the dissolved oxygen. That particular science lesson does lend itself to a practical storage method for the rare occasion that you have a metal find with organic material, such as wood or textile, attached. If allowed to dry out, organic material is likely to quickly disintegrate so the best way of preserving it in the short term is to keep it in a 'Wet Box'. Ideally this should be a clear plastic box with an airtight lid. It is fairly easy to keep objects wet, so most plastic food containers will suffice. Simply place your find in a labelled perforated bag and keep it covered in reasonably pure water; preferably boiled distilled or deionised water that has cooled before you use it. If the material floats, weigh it down with some inert material like pebbles. Change the water fortnightly to discourage bacterial and algae growth. You can keep this process going indefinitely but if you want to permanently take your find out of the 'Wet Box' you will need to seek advice from your Finds Liason Officer or local museum on the best way of more permanently conserving your find as, unfortunately, conservation of organic materials is a specialist job that cannot really be done at home.

While I haven't actually found anything with organic material attached that required wet storage, I have made a couple of finds from deep estuarine mud that amply demonstrates how well the exclusion of oxygen preserves finds. Twenty years ago I recovered an 1893 penny, which, after no more than a thorough washing in water, looked to be in near mint condition and has remained so until this day simply stored in a coin album in normal ambient conditions.

CM

1893 penny

Ten years ago I recovered another penny, some 850 years older, which again has only been washed before being stored in a coin tray at home.

CM

**Edward the Confessor penny**

The other side of the coin, if you'll pardon the pun, is preservation by reduction or elimination of moisture, which can be achieved in a 'Dry Box', with considerably less maintenance issues. In 2005, York Archaeological Trust produced a set of Conservation Advice Notes on behalf of the Portable Antiquities Scheme (PAS), which extolled the virtues of using a 'Dry Box' to halt corrosion of metals. You can download a copy here: http://finds.org.uk/conservation and the accompanying recommended parts list here: http://finds.org.uk/documents/file/drybox-leaflet.pdf or ask your Finds Liaison Officer for copies. Although the 'Dry Box' is undoubtedly a great idea, it doesn't seem to have caught on, for the only detectorist I know, who has a 'Dry Box', is me! I have to say that I have found my 'Dry Box' to be invaluable, for if I find a metal object in a perilous state then I can preserve it 'as is' until I can deal with it. There is also the added advantage that ten finds can often be treated in the same time as one, so I can safely save up finds needing the same treatment and deal with them as a batch, thus saving time and money. I have even won a great find from an archaeological dig as I was the only one involved who had the preservation facility it desperately needed.

I think there are two reasons the 'Dry box' has been largely ignored. Firstly it is human nature to prefer cure to prevention: everyone would buy a ladder to climb out of the big hole they just fell into but few would buy a fence so they didn't fall into the hole in the first place! The second reason is that, because of minimum order quantities, the recommended 'Dry Box' kit is a shopping list of largely, difficult to obtain, fairly expensive items for the average detectorist.

Let's take another look at the 'Dry Box'. In essence all you need is a large (five litre to ten litre) airtight clear polythene food storage container, desiccant to dry the air and a means of indicating Relative Humidity. I should explain that Relative Humidity (RH) is the measurement of the percentage of moisture content in air: 0% RH is bone dry; 100% RH is saturated. The ambient or normal humidity inside most buildings will usually be 50% RH with a variance of 10% or so, either way. According to studies, copper-alloys will not corrode below 35% RH, nor will iron kept below 15% RH.

The PAS recommended airtight polythene box, is the 7.5 litre Stewart Sealfresh Rectangular Meat Storer, cat no.1780008. Of all the boxes in all the World this seems the most elusive and expensive to obtain. Stewart themselves sell in bulk to retailers, so would want a very large order. I obtained a list of retailers from them only to find that my listed local retailer did not sell Stewart products and the largest food storer they had was a meagre three litres. The best price I could find for a single box was £14.00, including postage, from Amazon. Azpack: http://www.storeanddisplay.co.uk (tel: 01509 261256) will supply a pack of four Stewart boxes, which work out at £8.00 each, including delivery, so that is a reasonable option for a club or group.

Five years ago I bought a 'Dry Box' kit from a metal detector dealer (a couple of dealers were selling these at the time). The box itself was a Whitefurze brand six litre canister (cat no. F0750) and this has stood the test of time, so I wouldn't hesitate to recommend this brand as an alternative to Stewart. Whitefurze (http://www.whitefurze.net tel: 02476 717755) again supply in bulk but may be able to advise a local retailer. I did find a seven litre Whitefurze square container (cat no. F0460) at Morrisons supermarket for £2.50 but although it will do the job, its 12mm height will only just accommodate the common grip-top finds bags stood vertically, if the top of the bags are folded over; 14mm high or a little more is better. There were several offers of

Whitefurze containers on the Internet and I bought a 10 litre square food storage box, (cat no. F0450) on Ebay, for £6.40, including delivery.

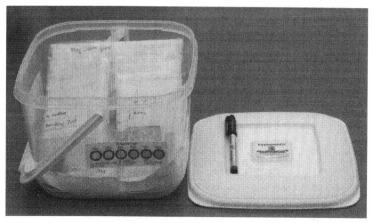

**Dry Box based on Whitefurze six-litre canister**

The other essential is desiccant to dry the air in the container and Silica Gel beads, which absorb moisture from their surroundings and release it again when heated, are normally used for this. Silica Gel comes in non-indicating and self-indicating form, which warns you by colour change when it has ceased functioning and needs drying out. It used to be a simple case of blue when dry and pink when wet but it is now more environmentally friendly to have orange dry and dark green or colourless when wet – it doesn't matter as long as we know what the colours mean. Silica Gel is widely available in varying quantities but 100 gram bags are probably the best for our purposes and we need around 90 grams per litre of container, plus or minus a couple of bags. GeeJay Chemicals www.geejaychemicals.co.uk/contactus.htm (tel: 01767 682774), are a traditional supplier of Silica Gel bags and will sell direct to home users but for seasoned Internet shoppers there are plenty of lower cost alternatives such as Ebay.

At first sight self-indicating Silica Gel would appear to be the best buy but the slight problem with it is that it doesn't begin to change colour until the environment contains more moisture than is good for storing metal finds. If you are not storing iron and keep a very close watch on your box, you may get away with just the self-indicating Silica Gel but really, to be safe, you need a humidity indicator.

The traditional indicator is a six spot card, where the spots reversibly change colour from pink to blue or green to brown at 10% rises in Relative Humidity. These cards are normally about £1.50 each and sold in minimum quantities of 10, although I did manage to buy a pack of 10 on Ebay for £3.74, including postage. GeeJay Chemicals (see above) sell them in addition to Silica Gel. There is now an alternative, which is a battery operated mini digital LCD thermometer, and humidity reader priced from below £2.00 on Ebay and Amazon. These clearly require more maintenance than an indicator card and could fail completely but I am quite happy to use one alongside self-indicating Silica Gel. Humidity indicators should be taped inside the box, facing outwards so that you can read them from the outside without removing the lid.

Now that you have your 'Dry Box', if you wish, you can just put the odd find in that needs preserving, as is but to make a more useful and safe storage system a quantity of small polythene bags would be useful. Bank coin bags would do but the grip-top write-on type; internal size 3.5in (8.9cm) x 4.5in (11.4cm) would be far better. The bags need perforating to allow moisture to escape so to perforate your empty bag you can use a standard two-hole paper punch and punch it once on each of the two vertical edges of the bag, which will add eight holes in total. You will find it much easier to punch the holes if you slide a piece of scrap thin card in the punch underneath and supporting the bag. As the number of finds in the box grows you do not want to have finds sitting on top of one another as the pressure from above could damage finds underneath and also trap moisture. The bags need some cushioning material such as Jiffy closed-cell polythene foam or acid-free tissue paper inserted to protect the find and encourage the bag to stand upright. Ideally one sheet of 4mm Jiffy foam cut to fit the internal dimensions of the bag will do the job. You could also use two or three sheets of thinner Jiffy foam or ten sheets of acid-free tissue paper. Both Jiffy foam and acid-free tissue is available from stationers and packaging suppliers. You may need to shop around for Jiffy foam as it is usually sold in large rolls although I have been able to buy small quantities on Ebay as well as saving any that is packed around goods arriving in my mail.

The conservationists say that all you should do to your finds is to let them dry out at room temperature (not on radiators or in ovens as they may shatter) on white kitchen towel, unwashed, and then put them in the 'Dry Box'. This is because washing can cause further corrosion and damage or lose fragile plating, inlay or associated organic material. Most detecting finds are fairly robust and having made an initial assessment, I prefer to carefully wash my finds so I know what I am dealing with. I don't believe one more soaking will do any harm to something that has lain in damp ground for aeons and there will be slightly less volume to keep dry.

You then need to put your find in the perforated grip-top polythene bag, with Jiffy foam or acid-free tissue paper inserted and label the bag with a permanent marker. Write the find details on the bag, slide the Jiffy foam or acid-free tissue paper in, followed by the find itself, seal the bag so your find doesn't fall out, add the complete package to your 'Dry Box' and replace the lid securely. All you need to do then is to store the box away from strong sunlight and check the

RH indicator now and again. As the Silica Gel absorbs moisture and loses efficiency the electronic device registers a rise in RH, while the panels on the indicator strip, progressively change colour, traditionally from blue to pink but on some types, brown to pale green. If you are storing iron then you need to dry out the Silica Gel as soon as the RH rises or when it reaches 30% for other metals. Check all the finds in the box for any problems at the same time.

I found that the Silica Gel in my 'Dry Box' only needed drying out once every two years! But it all depends on how much you use your box as every time you take the lid off, damp air will flood in and shorten the period. Regenerating the Silica Gel can be done in a number of ways, the easiest being to place the bags in a warm airing cupboard or on top of a continuously warm radiator for a couple of days. You will know that the Silica Gel has dried out completely if you weigh the bags at intervals during drying until there is no further weight loss. With these methods you could dry half the bags at a time so that you maintain a reasonably dry atmosphere for your finds in the box.

There are quicker and more aggressive methods of drying the Silica Gel involving the oven or microwave but beware that the Silica Gel gets very hot; synthetic bags may melt and glued bag seams can fail. If the Silica Gel can be removed from its bag, tip it out into an appropriate open top ovenproof or microwavable container or put the whole bag into such a container if the bag is sealed, either way you can recover the Silica Gel at the end of the operation.

Place the Silica Gel in an oven on very slow heat 110-120° C; (225-250° F; gas mark ¼-½) for up to several hours to evaporate off the moisture. If you are using a gas oven be careful not to set fire to the bags containing the Silica Gel. After one hour, weigh the Silica Gel bags on your kitchen scales and note the weight, then return them to the oven for a further hour and reweigh. If there is no loss in weight then the bags are completely dry and can be returned to the 'Dry Box', if there is weight loss, note the weight and return them to the oven for another hour. Repeat the process until there is no further weight loss. If you want to use the microwave, heat the Silica Gel on full power for one minute, then rest for one minute, check the weight and repeat until there is no further weight loss. A hundred grams of Silica Gel usually dries out in about five minutes.

## 8.1. Cleaning Finds

Before you start any form of cleaning you really need to try and identify the object and have some idea of its historic and monetary value. Coin collectors & dealers will probably tell you that a coin can be reduced to a tenth of its monetary value by cleaning, although you rarely see coins for sale covered in muck and corrosion unless they are being sold specifically as uncleaned. Sometimes it can be a Catch 22 situation where an object has little value because it cannot be identified for lack of cleaning but cleaning reduces the value to a fraction of what it would have been, if it hadn't been cleaned in the first place. However, it is a good idea to try and identify and value everything before you start cleaning and you'll know what you stand to lose if it goes wrong or whether it is worthwhile paying for a professional conservator to carry out the task. Potential treasure objects are not a problem, do not clean them, just report them and hand them in and if they are disclaimed and returned to you, you can deal with them then, with the benefit of a clear identification.

I only have space to give a brief guide to cleaning, it is, after all, a fairly large subject and each find may need different treatment from the next. Firstly, safety should be paramount. Follow all instructions in the safe use of substances and equipment. In particular:

* Accidents do happen- keep fresh clean water and preferably an eye bath handy.

* Wear an apron or coverall to protect clothes and body.

* Keep children and pets out of the working area.

* Dispose of discarded chemicals and solutions responsibly.

* Avoid drinking, eating and smoking in the working area.

* Wear a dust mask when handling powders and removing deposits from metals.

* Electricity and water do not mix – take care.

* Wear eye protection and surgical type gloves.

* Some chemicals and processes are flammable – avoid naked flames.

* Mop up spillages immediately.

* Use tongs and tweezers to handle objects in and out of solutions.

* Use all tools as intended and follow manufacturer's and supplier's safety advice.

* Ensure adequate ventilation.

* Wash hands thoroughly after handling chemicals and objects.

* Avoid contaminating kitchen worktops and cooking utensils.

## Mechanical cleaning

Good hands-free magnification is essential for most mechanical cleaning and, except for very gentle cleaning with a cotton-bud (Q-tip) or wooden cocktail stick, only robust finds should be subjected to mechanical cleaning.

In its basic form mechanical cleaning is carried out with manual handtools such as scalpels dental picks, ink erasers and glass fibre or wire pen brushes. For larger heavily corroded pieces you could use an oscillating engraver such as the Dremel 290.

Whatever tool you are using the method is basically the same. The object is best firmly held and supported in a machine vice, which will also prevent damaged fingers. The jaws should be soft rubber covered (or use chamois leather if the jaws are steel) to protect the object being held and also supported beneath with a strip of wood. Start no more than a millimetre in from the edge of the corrosion and apply light vertical pressure and the edge of the corrosion will break off. (Excessive pressure will dent or pit the surface of the metal underneath as will any pressure applied with electric engravers – let the tool do the work). Move not more than another millimetre in and repeat the process. If you move the tool too far in from the edge of the corrosion, it puts an enormous strain on the object, which could shatter. As the corrosion dust builds up it should be periodically removed with a very soft bristle artist's brush or a blower brush used for camera lenses. Do not be tempted to scrape the dust off using the tool that you are breaking the corrosion off with. Obviously any corrosion left after brushing off will need to be tackled as previously. It is a slow painstaking process but eventually the job will be finished and you should be pleased with the results.

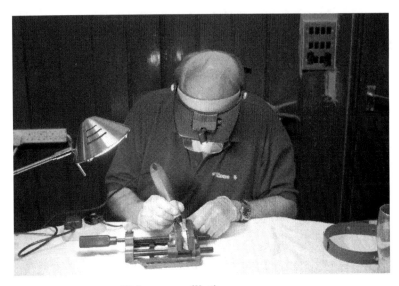

**Using an oscillating engraver**

More mechanised cleaning can be carried out with an ultrasonic cleaner or barrelling machine.

## Ultrasonic cleaner

The ultrasonic cleaner consists of a tank through which ultrasonic waves (usually from 15-400 kHz) are passed. The object (or objects, providing they don't overlap one another) to be cleaned is placed in the tank, which is partially filled with warm water at around 50°C to which a drop or two of washing-up liquid can be added to lower the surface tension of the water. The washing-up liquid effectively makes water 'wetter', allowing better penetration of the surface detail of the object. The cleaner runs on a timed cycle during which the sound waves cause energy to be released through cavitation or the generation and collapse of millions of microscopic bubbles, which breaks up dirt and contaminants from the object, usually in a few minutes. Ultrasonic cleaners are readily available from some metal detector dealers, electronic retailers, jewellery trade and hobby suppliers and even some supermarkets.

Providing they are used with care, these cleaners are probably the most useful mechanical cleaner available. They have a double use in that they can remove dirt and corrosion in their own right without the use of harsh chemicals and can also be used to thoroughly wash a find particularly after it has been chemically treated.

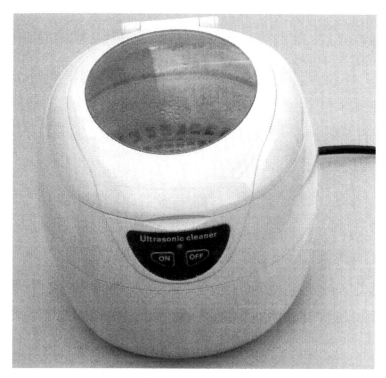

**Ultrasonic cleaner**

## Barrelling machine

Barrelling machines, available from many metal detector retailers, consist of an electrically driven internally finned plastic drum into which you seal up to ten or so objects to be cleaned, with steel shapes, soap and water. Typically the cleaning cycle is around four hours. I have used one of these machines, the same one, for more than thirty years and although I have gone through a number of drive belts and drum caps that machine is still going strong.

Barrelling is very harsh and, depending on the length of treatment, polishes metal to a satin or bright finish, removing surface metal in the process and also any plating, inlay or enamel. Older finds may come out pitted as the process scours out deeply embedded corrosion, so this treatment is best used for the bulk treatment of robust modern finds such as modern coinage and brass badges. Special burnishing soap is sold by barrelling machine suppliers and this is designed to be used at the rate of around one tablespoon per charge, to give the best polish effect for army badges and the like. A tablespoon of pure soap flakes or a squirt of washing up liquid can be used instead if a high lustre isn't necessary.

**Barrelling machine**

## Electrolysis

Electrolysis involves the passing of a low voltage direct electric current (DC) through the object to be cleaned and a dilute chemical solution called an electrolyte, in which the object is suspended. The object to be cleaned forms the negative electrode or cathode, while the other side of the circuit, the positive electrode or anode is scrap stainless steel; the corrosion removed being passed into solution as well as being redeposited on the anode. Electrolysis works by releasing hydrogen gas from the water at the cathode, which attacks and gradually eliminates the corrosion.

If you thought barrelling was harsh, electrolysis is mega harsh and definitely a last resort – the last drink in the last chance saloon! Electrolysis can strip to bare metal in minutes, which may be okay for silver but not so good for copper-alloys. Plating, inlays and enamels will definitely be lost. The act of passing electricity through metals physically alters their structure and I have seen lumps of corrosion on silver objects reduced to solid silver so you can end up with a silver object covered in silver warts and the process is irreversible. Some ancient bronze objects contain quantities of lead, which is distributed in globules and selectively removed by electrolysis leaving ugly pits. Not only that but the removed lead goes into solution and can plate the bronze. You have been warned! However, if you have a heavily encrusted object and no other way of cleaning it and you are prepared to risk total loss, electrolysis may just produce wonderful results. It is also quite suitable for lead and lead alloys where their softness tends to preclude mechanical cleaning.

There are also three personal hazards to be aware of in the use of electrolysis, the main being the use of electricity with water. The electrolysis 'tank' should be stood within a suitable plastic tray, while the power source should remain outside the tray or in its own smaller tray within the main tray providing it is of sufficient depth to protect the power source from total spillage of the tank. The second hazard is that hydrogen gas is given off which is not only inflammable but readily forms explosive mixtures with air, which apparently can happen inside the body, so good ventilation no smoking, nor naked flames etc. Finally, because of the escape of gas the electrolyte can splash and it may become more harmful as the cleaning proceeds.

Again some metal detector dealers sell 'switch on and go' electrolysis kits, which undoubtedly work and are usually supplied with everything you need to get started (except perhaps water and a clothes peg). You can however, build your own kit fairly easily. The main part is a transformer, usually called an adaptor, with an output of up to 12 volts DC. You will also need a plastic container of around a litre capacity, a couple of crocodile clips (preferably a red one and a black one), a clothes peg and a piece of scrap stainless steel (e.g. cutlery). If you haven't found any stainless steel and can't find any redundant in the kitchen, try a charity or thrift shop.

It is preferable to have a transformer or adaptor with a means of varying the voltage, which gives much more control of the process. Maplin Electronics supply a range of variable voltage AC (mains) adaptors, which have switch selectable outputs of 3, 4.5, 6, 7.5, 9 & 12 volts DC. There are a number of current ratings and all will work but aim for 1000mA – 1500mA (1Amp – 1.5Amps), which will be fairly robust and less likely to trip out on thermal overload during prolonged use. Although it is overkill for our purpose, you could also use a car battery charger with dual voltage, 6 & 12 VDC output. If you have a spare adaptor in the 4.5v – 12v range you can always start with that but don't use one you need for anything else as you will have to cut the output plug, or power tip, off. You will have to do the same with the Maplin adaptor. Most adaptors have two wires (their sleeves are lightly welded together) on the output side, one all black, which should be the negative, the other black and white, which should be the positive. Get your adaptor and remove the power tip by cutting through the output wiring with pliers, as close to the power tip as possible. Pull the two wires apart for about four inches and strip off the end half inch of insulation or sleeve on each wire. Twist each of the bare wire ends to consolidate the strands. Fill your plastic container with water and place the two bare wire ends in the water a few inches apart making sure they don't touch. Plug in your adaptor, switch on and look carefully at the wires in the water, one of them should be fizzing, write down the colour or mark that wire with a piece of tape to identify it. That should be the black wire but nevertheless fix the black crocodile clip to it and fix the red crocodile clip to the other wire.

Electrolysis cleaners can work extraordinarily well but the one area where they leave a lot to be desired is the method for attaching the object to be cleaned. The usual method is to hold the object in a crocodile clip, which has to bite through the corrosion to make an electrical connection often scarring the object in the process. Also the crocodile clips are usually plated steel which quickly corrode; brass would be better but they are very uncommon nowadays. Another method is to make a hanger from stiff bare copper wire, which is slightly better but can still scratch the object. My solution is to use 28mm copper pipe clips (spacing), which can be bent to grip the object, particularly a coin, safely on its edge after first brushing the contact area with a glassfibre brush to ensure a good connection. Avoid using the brush on other types of object though.

To make the holder using pipe clips you will need to take two of the smaller spacers and join one each side of a larger clip using brass nuts and bolts, then remodel the pliable spacers so that they hook over each side of the plastic container. The central clip can be adjusted to hold different sized objects. Eventually the parts used in the solution will disintegrate, so hold on to the other clips, spacers, nuts and bolts, that inevitably come in small packs, so you can repair and remake holders as required.

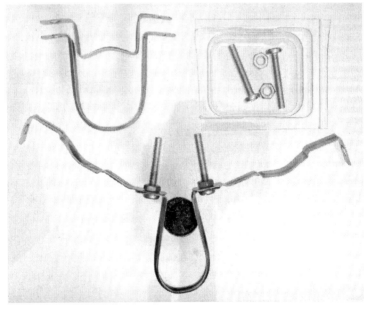

**Holder made from pipe clip and spacers**

The current popular electrolyte is citric acid and salt solution. I think it is a good idea to avoid salt but if you want to use citric acid make up a 1% solution (10 grams in a litre of pure water) and you will have to add half a teaspoon of salt to get the current to flow. I prefer to use a 5% solution (50 grams in one litre of pure water) of either sodium carbonate (washing soda), sodium bicarbonate (baking soda) or better still for copper-alloys, a 50/50 mixture of the two which is equivalent to sodium sesquicarbonate. There is a high risk of unwanted plating occurring if different metals are cleaned in the same solution so two separate tanks, one for silver cleaning and a second for base metals would be ideal. Alternatively a good wash-up would be necessary when changing from one metal to another. Electrolyte can be stored in labelled plastic bottles for reuse until it gets very dirty, when a fresh batch should be made up. If you have two tanks made from plastic containers with lids, you can remove the electrodes and store the electrolyte in the tank with the lid on.

Cleaning is achieved by mounting the object in the cathode or negative clamp (black) and ensuring it is completely submerged in the electrolyte. Ensure the transformer is turned OFF and clip the stainless steel anode to the inside of the plastic tank with a clothes peg so that it is touching the bottom of the tank, a few inches away from but directly opposite the object and partly submerged in the electrolyte. Connect the transformer or adaptor to a suitable 13-amp mains socket and turn it on at low voltage say 4.5 volts, if you have that option. Gradually increase the voltage as necessary until you see a steady stream of small bubbles coming from the object. The newer Maplin adaptors have to be unplugged from wall sockets to change the voltage so carefully remove the cathode complete with object out of the solution and return once the voltage is changed and the power is back on. If there are no bubbles, assuming the hardware is wired up and working correctly, carefully move the cathode, nearer to the stainless steel anode. If bubbling becomes very vigorous, back off the voltage or move the cathode further from the anode. The amount of electrolysis required varies very much from object to object but err on the side of caution and start with just one minute. After a minute, carefully remove the object (avoid touching the anode with the object as this could damage the transformer or adaptor) then turn off the power. If you turn off the power first, there is a great risk of the object becoming plated. Wipe the object gently with a wet paper towel, tissue or toothbrush, then rinse in clean water. Carefully examine the object to assess the degree of cleaning achieved and if further electrolysis is required, resume cleaning for another minute followed by a wet wipe and further checking. If little or no cleaning has occurred, double-up on the time between checks and keep doubling until you get results (e.g. 2 minutes, 5 minutes, 10 minutes, 20 minutes etc.); some objects take several hours. Once the object has been cleaned enough, put it to soak and rest in pure water for 24 hours. Always remove and clean the anode before commencing cleaning the next object, even if it is the same metal and if the electrolyte level has dropped through evaporation, top-up with pure water.

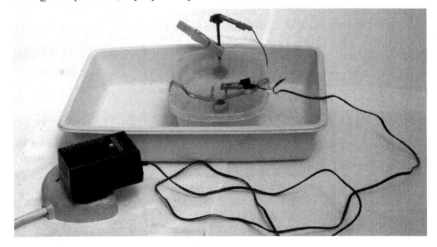

**Electrolysis**

## Chemical cleaning

Most of the chemicals we'll be using are domestic, so in themselves they are not too obnoxious, however we will often be using them in ways they weren't really intended to be used in the home and that could give rise to problems. I will point out the known dangers but be aware that the corrosion products and hence the chemistry will undoubtedly differ from object to object and there might be nasty surprises. Only use these treatments if you are confident in doing so and whatever you do, please take precautions. At least wear waterproof gloves and eye protection and handle chemicals carefully at arm's length so any spitting or splashing is away from your face.

As the chemistry of every object will differ, there is not going to be one right way and one wrong way to clean a particular object. It will be very much a case of trial, error, experience and personal preference. Under-cleaning is preferable to over-cleaning. Slow and steady wins the race and shortcuts lead to long delays. Bear in mind that there is nothing at all wrong with doing a bit of chemical cleaning, which will loosen and soften encrustation then switching to mechanical cleaning or even electrolysis then back to chemical cleaning and so on until the job is done. All we want is good results, which should get even better with practice.

If you have localised areas of corrosion it is better to dab the chemical onto the area with a cotton bud so that the chemical only works where it is needed. However, more often than not, corrosion covers the whole object and soaking is

112

necessary if you are going to use chemical treatments. So to get started we need a few small plastic containers with lids to minimise evaporation so the solution won't increase in strength or dry out over time, the smallest of the food container range (150-200 ml) will be about right. Label the containers with the solution name in permanent marker on the side and on the lid so you know exactly what is where and there won't then be any mishaps. I'm sure you will realise that you only need to cover the object completely with the solution, it is not necessary to fill the container.

All references to 'pure water' means the best quality water you can obtain, ideally it should be distilled water but as that is now quite difficult to get hold of, de-ionised water is quite acceptable.

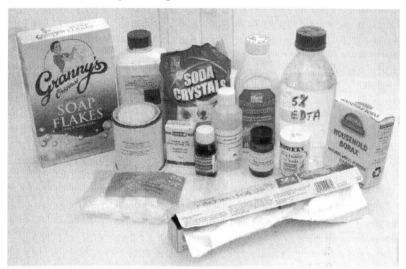

**A selection of cleaning chemicals**

## Making solutions

Nearly all the chemicals that are used for cleaning are supplied in solid form and need to be dissolved in a liquid (usually pure water) before they can be used. The technique is fairly simple once you've tried it a couple of times and all you need is an accurate weighing device measuring in grams and a means of measuring volume, preferably in millilitres (ml) but centilitres (10 ml) or even decilitres (100 ml) will suffice. You may come across the volumetric measurement: cubic centimetre (cc) which is exactly the same as a millilitre. If you are buying chemicals from a metal detector dealer you will usually be supplied with a quality plastic storage bottle and instructions. Some of the chemicals we will be using are domestic and come as they are. Washed-out plastic milk containers, while not being the strongest, are readily available in

113

useful one pint or half litre (500ml) and two pint or one litre (1000ml). If you want smaller containers then soft drinks bottles are quite usable in 250ml and 330 ml. It is vital, for your own sake and everyone around you, that you clearly re-label any domestic containers you use with the precise contents in permanent marker.

The main solutions we will be making up are solids dissolved in liquid at a weight to volume ratio (w/v). The concentration is given in percent, which means the number of grams dissolved in 100 millilitres of liquid. Not the number of grams dissolved in a litre, which is 1000 millilitres. For example a 5% solution is 5 grams in 100 ml; 10 grams in 200ml; 12.5 grams in 250 ml; 25 grams in 500ml and 50 grams in a litre. I'm sure you can pro-rata any other percentages and volumes from that. Using milk containers, which have wide necks, it is quite easy to pour the solid into the container via a rolled up sheet of paper made into a funnel and then to add liquid up to the half litre or litre mark as appropriate. You then put the top on and shake until the solid is dissolved. I wouldn't worry if some of the solid doesn't dissolve as it will probably do so, eventually, of its own accord. Warming water beforehand will help the solid dissolve faster but it is highly dangerous to warm flammable solvents like alcohol.

A few solutions are liquid diluted with another liquid at a volume to volume ratio (v/v). This is similar to the above except the percentage is a measure of the number of millilitres in 100 millilitres. For example a 5% solution is 5 millilitres in 100 ml; 10 millilitres in 200ml; 12.5 millilitres in 250 ml; 25 millilitres in 500ml and 50 millilitres in a litre.

If you want to change the concentration of an existing solution you can add a measured amount of the appropriate solid to make it stronger, e.g. to make a litre of 5% solution into a litre of 10% solution, add 50 grams of the appropriate solid and dissolve. To reduce the concentration of an existing solution just add a measured amount of water or appropriate solvent, e.g. to reduce 500ml of 10% solution to 5%, add 500ml of water or appropriate solvent which will make a litre of solution at 5% concentration.

Before we start, the important thing to remember about chemical cleaning is that over time the solution and the object will reach equilibrium where either the active ingredient is neutralised or all used up or the solution becomes saturated with contaminants and can't absorb any more. Often there will be a physical change where the solution becomes dirty or changes colour and sometimes there can be harmful by-products so it is necessary to regularly discard the used solution and replace with fresh. As a rule of thumb: if there is no noticeable change to the object being cleaned or the solution over a period of 24 hours, then renew the solution; if this produces no change over the next 24 hours, then change the treatment.

1. Pure water – all metals except iron. If we have to clean, the mildest treatment we can give any non-ferrous metal object is to soak it in pure water. Soak it for about 24 hours and if the water is dirty it is doing a job so change the water and repeat the process. It is fine to brush the object gently with a soft brush or for fragile objects roll a cotton bud over between soaks, the more dirt and debris we can take off, the better.

2. Soap solution – all metals except iron. Most washing up liquids and powders contain additives, which may be harmful. Teepol make a neutral laboratory grade liquid detergent if you can get hold of it (bear in mind Teepol make formulations for the domestic market which will be no different for our purposes than other brands). The best you can probably do is to buy pure soap flakes from a supermarket etc. and make up a 0.5% solution (5 grams in a litre of pure water). It is quite difficult to dissolve the soap flakes so it is best to heat up the water in a kettle (don't get it too hot or your plastic container will melt, let the water cool a little before you use it, if necessary). If you use Teepol the recommended concentration will be 5 ml in a litre of pure water). Soak your object for 24 hours and check and brush it etc. All the while dirt is coming off, keep soaking. This treatment may be all that is required for lightly soiled objects but once you have finished the treatment you will need to remove the soap residue so to do that you go back and repeat stage 1. Pure water, until all evidence of soap, bubbles etc. has been removed.

3. Sodium hexametaphosphate (SHMP) – mainly copper-alloys. A non-corrosive chemical for rapidly removing dirt and corrosion deposits from copper-alloys, while, with care, keeping the patina intact. Use a 10% solution (100 grams in a litre of pure water), soak for ten minutes and then brush or swab off in pure water. Repeat as necessary but beware SHMP will eventually strip the object down to bare metal. Then see: 'After cleaning treatment'.

4. Acid Treatment – all metals. This is just one route of treatment, which will suit the olive oil and lemon juice brigades. As you have probably guessed, I am not going to recommend either of those natural, or fairly natural, substances. Olive oil is very mildly acidic at 0.3% to 3%, depending on factors such as where the olives are grown, it is also a variable mixture of ingredients, so you won't know what is in the mixture and cleaning results will vary from one bottle to the next. Worse than that, oil is very difficult to near impossible to remove from objects and can trap moisture with the effect that corrosion continues or worsens. The main active ingredient of lemon juice is citric acid, which varies between 4.5% and about 10% and again contains a variable mixture of substances, so your cleaning results will vary from lemon to lemon. Bottled lemon juice is probably more consistent but on the other hand contains additives, which may be harmful to finds.

What I am going to propose is that you use citric acid crystals, which are available from some metal detector dealers and, being used in home wine and beer making, are readily available from high street chemists etc. As a substitute for olive oil use a 1% citric acid solution (10 grams in a litre of pure water), which will soften encrustation for mechanical removal as well as gently cleaning objects in their own right. You can leave the object in soak for a few days up to a few weeks. You will need to mechanically remove any lumps of corrosion and to turn the object over every day or so to even out the cleaning on both sides. If the solution stops working before all the corrosion has been removed, it would be prudent to replace the solution, as the acid will have become exhausted.

As a substitute for lemon juice use a 5% citric acid solution (50 grams in a litre of pure water) and this works well on all metals (particularly copper-alloys and silver alloys showing green corrosion), including iron, as citric acid is used commercially for rust removal. These citric acid solutions will strip down to bare metal eventually and may attack the metal itself so their best use is as a corrosion softener to aid mechanical cleaning. If cleaning is happening too fast, just dilute the solution down until you are happy with the results. Then see: 'After cleaning treatment'.

5. Jeweller's stock – mainly silver and precious metals. I'm not a great fan of potions but this is a traditional jewellery cleaner made up from fairly readily obtainable household cleaning chemicals, which apart from ammonia fumes (irritant, so make and use in a well-ventilated area), aren't too obnoxious. All the chemicals are available at supermarkets, pound stores, hardware stores, chemists, etc. For a litre of solution you will need:

Household Borax – 13grams

Washing Soda – 6 grams

Pure Soap Flakes – 5 grams

Household Ammonia (9.5%) – 85 millilitres

Pure Water – 915 millilitres

This is probably a similar formula to 'Silver Dip' and will remove tarnish and corrosion from silver and gold without appearing to attack the metal but use sparingly and swab or soak for 10 minutes at a time. It could also be used on copper-alloys but it strips down to bare metal very fast. Then see: 'After cleaning treatment'.

6. Sodium bicarbonate and aluminium foil – silver. The black tarnish often found on silver is silver sulphide, which can be removed by setting up an electrochemical reaction with aluminium foil and an alkaline solution. Sodium

bicarbonate is called by other names such as bicarbonate of soda, bicarb or baking soda (not baking powder which is a mixture of sodium bicarbonate and tartaric acid). Other alkalis such as sodium carbonate (washing soda) or saliva can be used but will not work as well as sodium bicarbonate and what's more I dread to think what you might have had in your mouth.

The method works wonderfully well for coins as it tends to brighten the high spots and leave the lower parts darker so you achieve a contrast allowing features and legends to be easily identified. Cut a piece of baking foil large enough to wrap the object, lay the object on the foil, wet the object with 5% sodium bicarbonate solution (50 grams in a litre of pure water) and wrap the foil around the object smoothing the foil with your fingers. Heat is generated in the reaction and hydrogen sulphide gas is given off, which apart from smelling of bad eggs is a toxic and inflammable gas, so good ventilation is needed but naked flames and lighted cigarettes definitely aren't! Repeat the process as many times as necessary to achieve the desired result. If necessary you can screw the aluminium into a loose ball and gently rub the blackened areas, however there is a risk of scratching the object and it might be better to use electrolysis for any object not responding to the foil wrapping treatment. Then see: 'After cleaning treatment'. The object can be gently polished with a silver polishing cloth afterwards if desired.

7. Sodium thiosulphate – silver mainly but can be used on copper-alloys. The principal use for sodium thiosulphate is in traditional photographic development as a fixative, so it is available from photographic suppliers and often called 'hypo'. As it is used in photography to remove silver halides, it can be used effectively to remove silver chloride (a halide) or horn silver, which shows as a purple-grey to dark grey crust on silver objects. Swab or soak the object in a 5% sodium thiosulphate solution (100 grams in a litre of pure water) for ten minutes then check and gently brush the object. Repeat as necessary. Then see: 'After cleaning treatment'. Silver objects can be gently polished with a silver polishing cloth afterwards if desired.

8. Ethylene diamine tetra-acetic acid (EDTA) – mainly lead, lead alloys and iron. EDTA is usually supplied as its disodium or trisodium salt. It is excellent at dissolving metal oxides, particularly (white) lead oxide and iron oxide, better known as rust. It is available from some metal detector dealers and should be made up into a 5% solution (50 grams in a litre of pure water). Simply swab or soak the object until the deposits are dissolved. Then see: 'After cleaning treatment'.

9. Alcohol/Acetone – all metals. These solvents are used as supplied for degreasing, cleaning and drying of any metals and to dissolve some substances, which are near insoluble in water. All are highly inflammable and volatile, the fumes can be harmful if inhaled so use in a well-ventilated area, free from

117

naked flames, and keep containers tightly covered. Wear gloves when using solvents as oils in the skin can transfer back onto the object and the removal of oils from the skin may cause problems such as cracked skin. To use these solvents either brush it over the object thoroughly or soak for 20 minutes. These solvents can be a problem to get hold of. Mineralised Methylated Spirits (MMS) or Meths is the purple (shades vary) fluid readily available from hardware shops etc., however it contains pyridine, which will leave harmful deposits on metal objects, so only use MMS if you have a purer alcohol or acetone you can use for a final rinse. Industrial Methylated Spirits (IMS), now called Industrial Denatured Alcohol (IDA) does not contain pyridine and is widely used by conservators, however unless you are willing to pay about £20 per litre excise duty, you need to obtain a free licence from Customs and Excise, which will allow you to use up to 20 litres per year in your hobby, under section 17.8 of Production, distribution and use of denatured alcohol HMRC Notice 473 (July 2005).

Other alcohols you can use are Industrial Alcohol or rubbing alcohol, which is iso-propanol or iso-propyl alcohol (IPA) and methyl alcohol or methanol, which are free from customs restrictions. Acetone is not an alcohol but is also quite acceptable and is more widely available than IPA and methanol as it is commonly used for nail varnish remover, however there is a trend to make it more user-attractive by adding colour and perfume which we want to avoid for our purposes. The next problem is that Royal Mail won't transport solvents so you either need to collect from the supplier or find one that uses a suitable carrier. IPA and acetone are both used as solvents in glassfibre construction projects so are available from suppliers in this area such as yacht chandlers and some car accessory suppliers. Acetone is available at high street chemists.

After cleaning treatment – With the exception of the solvents just mentioned (other than MMS), it is essential that all remains of chemicals used are removed otherwise corrosion may continue or even get worse! If the object is robust and not plated, inlaid or enamelled and you have an ultrasonic cleaner, then you can give it a normal cycle in pure water in the cleaner but bear in mind that you may get bright spots on the object where it touches the tank. Otherwise you will need to soak it in soap solution and then soak it in pure water. Iron should not be put in water or soap solution, otherwise it will rust, and neither should any object that has been dried using solvents. Blot iron dry with white kitchen towel then soak for 20 minutes in alcohol (except MMS) or acetone to remove any remaining water and chemical.

# 9. Dowsing

An easy way of improving your metal detecting success is to learn to dowse. According to the British Society of Dowsers anyone can learn to dowse. Traditionally dowsing has been much used for finding water, however it can be used to find anything, unknown, lost, buried or hidden and so lends itself well to metal and mineral prospecting, treasure hunting and metal detecting. I personally have found dowsing invaluable in saving enormous amounts of time by avoiding areas barren of finds and by developing the technique of using just one dowsing rod I can guide my metal detector swiftly to good finds.

## The L-rod

While, as a generalisation, all dowsing tools can be used for all types of dowsing, a pendulum is best used for map dowsing and an L-rod for field dowsing. The basic L-rod is simply a length of stiff metal wire or thin round bar bent into the shape of the letter 'L', hence the name, although some might argue that it is an abbreviation of Locator Rod. Traditionally the short arm of the 'L' is held in a loose fist while the long arm projects forward over the top of the fist. There are a few variations on the basic design and my personal preference is one that British treasure dowser Jim Longton uses and has kindly allowed me to reproduce here. If you already have a pair of L-rods you are happy with, by all means use them or you can make excellent rods as follows:

You will need 22" (56cm) of round metal bar (brass is considered best) of diameter 1/16" (1.5mm) to 3/16" (5mm) to make each rod. Unless you have easy access to round bar, I suggest you use two wire coat hangers to begin with. (NB Measurements and angles do not need to be too precise to make a working rod):

*Invert the first hanger and measure 14" (36cm) from one side, along the horizontal bar then mark and cut through with a pair of pliers or a junior hacksaw. Measure 22" (56cm) back from the first cut and make a second cut. Discard the hooked portion. (Fig 1)

**Fig 1**

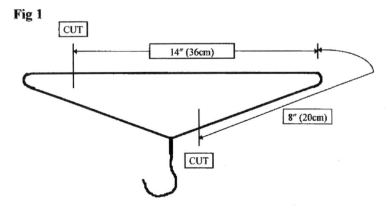

*Smooth the cut ends with a file or emery cloth.

*Using a pair of pliers or a vice, first straighten and then bend the shorter arm back to an angle of 135°. (Fig 2)

**Fig 2**

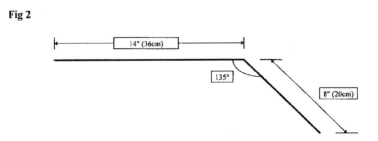

*Measure 7″ (18cm) along the shorter arm, from its end and bend this portion back until horizontal (Fig 3), then turn the last 5.5″ (14cm) up at right angles. Finally, turn the last 0.5″ (1cm) of the upright inwards, at right angles (Fig 4).

**Fig 3**

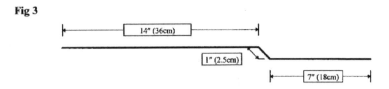

120

**Fig 4**

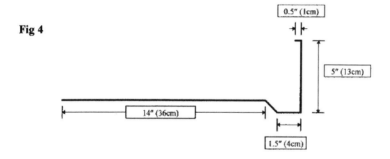

*Lay the rod on a level surface and adjust it until it lies reasonably flat.

*Make a second rod from the other coat hanger.

Health warning: The rods are perfectly harmless when used as described. If you wish to use them to play Conan the Barbarian, Robin Hood, Ivanhoe or act out any other fantasy, don't blame me if you puncture your eyeball or any other part of your body. I would suggest that children using the rods should be supervised by a responsible adult. The rods can be made extra safe by folding their tips downwards or back on themselves, wrapping their tips with insulating tape or applying a blob of a resin such as Araldite.

Holding the rods: Take the short arm of a rod in each hand so that the long arm is on the opposite side to your thumbs. Clench your fists around them loosely and turn your wrists so that your thumbs are uppermost and the long arm projects forward from the bottom of your fist. Tuck your elbows into your body and keep your upper arms in line with your body. Hold your forearms straight out in front of you, the width of your body apart and at whatever angle necessary to keep the rods reasonably parallel to the ground. The rods should now be pointing forward like extensions of your forearms. You may need to adjust your grip so that the rods are just free to move but not sloppy. When you are happy with holding the rods we can move on to some dowsing exercises:

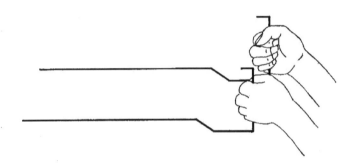

**Holding the rods**

Dowsing Excercises:

*Hold the rods in the normal dowsing position as just described. Ask the rods to turn left. After they have moved, restart the rods pointing forward. The easy way to get the rods to point forward is to drop your forearms so that the rods point to the ground, then raise your forearms back to the horizontal. Ask the rods to turn right. Restart. Ask the rods to cross. The rods will cross on your chest. Practise until the rods move easily.

*Place a coin on the floor then take a few paces back from it. Hold your rods in the normal dowsing position and walk slowly toward the coin saying: 'I am looking for a coin'. The rods will either cross as you pass immediately over the coin or within a few paces past the coin. Keep practising until the rods cross at the coin.

*Place a copper coin; a silver coin and a brass coin some distance apart on the ground. Hold your rods in the normal dowsing position and walk slowly toward the coin saying: 'I am looking for a copper coin'. The rods will cross as you pass over the copper coin but not the other two. Repeat the exercise with the silver coin and then the brass. Keep practising until you can differentiate between various metals.

*Stand sideways to a distant building or other large object that you know the location of and ask the rods to show you where it is. Give the full name of the place, i.e. 'Show me St. James' Church'. Clear your mind of everything else and concentrate. Once you get this to work, try standing with your back to the 'target' (as dowsers tend to call objects they are trying to find) and see what happens.

*When you have succeeded with the previous exercise, take your rods to the gate of a field or any other open space where you have any necessary search permission. Hold the rods as normal and ask: 'are there any coins buried in this field?' Normally the rods will cross for yes and move apart or open out for no.

122

You may need to determine what the rods' movement, or lack of it, means for you. Ask the rods to point to the nearest coin, then walk slowly in the direction indicated by the rods, turning, as necessary, to keep the rods pointing straight out in front of you. On reaching the coin the rods will cross. If you want to search for other objects as well as coins, ask the rods to find treasure.

*Keep practising. Once you can obtain a response from the rods in all these exercises, you are basically ready to do anything. Even if you can't do it all at first, you should find that the rods will produce some useful results in the field and you will improve with time.

You may have noticed that in the above exercise you located your first buried treasure but how do you recover it? It is almost essential to use a metal detector for final location of metallic objects, as pinpointing by dowsing alone is rarely precise. If you are looking for non-metallic treasures than that is a different ball game and unless you can devise your own pinpointing technique, presumably you are just going to have to dig for it. Returning to the exercises, using two rods leaves you no hands free to carry anything so, hopefully you will have brought someone else along, who can, at least, carry a metal detector and extraction tool, and perhaps do the digging for you. If you are the independent sort, you don't need to have a partner, it's very easy to both dowse and recover targets by yourself using a metal detector and one of the following methods.

*Dowse and mark first, detect and dig second. You will need a couple of dozen one to two feet (30-60cm) long plastic tent pegs or wooden plant canes and something in which to carry them on your back or hip. I use an archery quiver but I am sure most of you could make or adapt something for carrying the sticks. All you do then is dowse and mark where the rods cross by pushing a stick into the ground. When you run out of sticks, set your detector up and detect from stick to stick, collecting the sticks as you go, as well as the finds.

*You can dowse with just one rod, believe it or not. The great advantage with single rod dowsing is that you have one hand free to use a metal detector, so you can both dowse and detect simultaneously. All you have to do is to sweep with the detector using one hand while holding the rod in your other hand. Theoretically you should be able to just follow the rod from one good target to the next, by moving your body to keep the forearm of your dowsing hand in line with the rod. To recover what you detect you only have to find a means of carrying a digging tool, without using your hands. A tool-belt works fine.

While we are on the subject of recovery, I ought to mention some of the pitfalls. A metal detector will not be able to detect every target that you dowse. Dowsing goes far deeper than metal detectors. I have heard of match head sized silver objects, dowsed at depths of three feet and I have dowsed targets that only produced a signal from a detector after I had dug out a foot depth of soil first. You can, of course, just dig a hole wherever your rods indicate a target but, unless you are looking for something specific like a suspected cache, you are likely to find this approach counter productive as it could take a couple of hours to dig each hole. I fit the largest suitable search-head to my detector; if a search for a target doesn't produce a signal, I just leave it and go on to the next target. I couldn't have made the find anyway, had I only used a detector.

## 10. Bibliography and Resources

Krause, **World Coins,**

Paul Murawski, **Benet's Artefacts of England & the United Kingdom,** (Greenlight Publishing, 2003),

Henry R Palmer, **Observations on the Motions of Shingle Beaches,** (1834)

Spink, **Coins of England & the United Kingdom** (annual publication)

## 10.1. Great Books In Print From The Same Author

Available from your favourite online or offline bookseller.

THE SUCCESSFUL TREASURE HUNTER'S SECRET MANUAL: Discovering Treasure Auras in the Digital Age, Soft Cover, 152mm x 229mm, (6 x 9 inches) 102 pages, (CreateSpace, 2017) ISBN 9781540747815

THE SUCCESSFUL TREASURE HUNTER'S SECRET MANUAL: How to Use Modern Cameras to Locate Buried Metals, Gold, Silver, Coins, Caches... (E-Book)

CLEANING COINS & ARTEFACTS: Conservation * Restoration * Presentation, Soft Cover, 210mm x 146mm, (8.25 x 5.75 inches) 110 pages, (Greenlight Publishing, 2008) ISBN 978 1 897738 337

THE SUCCESSFUL TREASURE HUNTER'S ESSENTIAL COIN AND RELIC MANAGER: How to Clean, Conserve, Display, Photograph, Repair, Restore, Replicate and Store Metal Detecting Finds (E-Book)

PERMISSION IMPOSSIBLE: Metal Detecting Search Permission Made Easy, Soft Cover, 210mm x 146mm, (8.25 x 5.75 inches) 52 pages, (True Treasure Books, 2007) ISBN 978 0 9550325 3 0 (Also an E-Book)

SITE RESEARCH FOR DETECTORISTS, FIELDWALKERS & ARCHAEOLOGISTS, Soft Cover, 250mm x 190mm, (9.75 x 7.5 inches) 160 pages, (Greenlight Publishing, 2006) ISBN 1 897738 285

THE SUCCESSFUL TREASURE HUNTER'S ESSENTIAL SITE RESEARCH MANUAL: How to Find Productive Metal Detecting Sites, (E-Book)

SUCCESSFUL DETECTING SITES: Locate 1000s of Superb Sites and Make More Finds, Soft Cover, 250mm x 190mm, (9.75 x 7.5 inches) 238 pages, (Greenlight Publishing, 2007) ISBN 978 1 897738 306

THE ESSENTIAL GUIDE TO OLD, ANTIQUE AND ANCIENT METAL SPOONS, Soft Cover, 210mm x 146mm, 88 pages, (True Treasure Books, 2008) ISBN 978 0 9550325 4 7 (Also an E-Book)

DOWSING FOR TREASURE: The New Successful Treasure Hunter's Essential Dowsing Manual, Soft Cover, 152mm x 229mm, (6 x 9 inches) 96 pages, (CreateSpace, 2016) ISBN 9781518766060 (Also an E-Book)

MY ANCESTOR LEFT AN HEIRLOOM: Discovering Heirlooms and Ancestors Through the Metalwork They Left Behind, Soft Cover, 210mm x 146mm, (8.25 x 5.75 inches) 84 pages, (True Treasure Books, 2011) ISBN 978 0 9550325 6 1.

MY ANCESTOR LEFT AN HEIRLOOM: Hunting Family History and Genealogy Treasure Through Metal Detecting Finds (E-Book)

METAL DETECTING MADE EASY: A Guide for Beginners and Reference for All, Soft Cover, 210mm x 146mm, (8.25 x 5.75 inches) 128 pages, (True Treasure Books, 2014) ISBN 978 0 9550325 7 8 (Also an E-Book)

FAITHFUL ATTRACTION: How to Drive Your Metal Detector to Find Treasure (E-Book)

TOKENS & TRADERS OF KENT in the Seventeenth, Eighteenth & Nineteenth Centuries, Soft Cover, 215mm x 140mm, (8.5 x 5.5 inches) 112 pages, (True Treasure Books, 2015) ISBN 978 0 9550325 8 5 (Also an E-Book)

METAL DETECTING BENEFITS FOR LANDOWNERS (co-authored with Jacq le Breton), Soft Cover, 152mm x 229mm, (6 x 9 inches) 32 pages, (CreateSpace, 2016) ISBN 978-1537341118 (a booklet for European metal detectorists, to give to landowners as a deluxe calling card)

HOW TO FIND BRITAIN'S BURIED TREASURE HOARDS, Soft Cover, 297mm x 210mm, (11.75 x 8 inches) 152 pages, (Greenlight Publishing, 2017) ISBN 978 1 897738 62 7

# About The Author

David Villanueva Was Born In Birmingham, England in 1951 and grew up there. In the early 1970s his mother bought him a copy of Ted Fletcher's book **A Fortune Under Your Feet**, which inspired him to buy a metal detector – a Goldfinger BFO. The performance was very poor by current standards but it did find coins and David became hooked. A few months later he upgraded to a deeper-seeking pulse induction machine and became very fond of searching beaches, which were very productive of modern coins and jewellery at the time. In those early days David also took an interest in other forms of treasure hunting including dump digging, SCUBA diving, and gold panning.

Following a move to Whitstable in Kent, England, David took to nearby beaches with his trusty old Pulsedec, but quickly found that the machine was not well-suited to local conditions – the Pulsedec had no discrimination and there was plenty of iron around. He changed to a locally produced C-Scope 1220B, which worked well on the drier parts of the beaches, and this encouraged him to try out some inland sites. He joined a metal detecting club and also gained permission to search a small farm, making all manner of finds that previously he had only read about in treasure hunting magazines (hammered silver coins, for instance). Having long had a keen interest in history, David started researching his locality, which led to more productive sites to search and to write about in 17 books and the two British metal detecting magazines – Treasure Hunting and The Searcher – which have published more than two dozens of David's articles between them.

But it was a chance encounter with Britain's best treasure dowser, Jim Longton that supercharged David's treasure hunting. Jim, who had already dowsed his way to a Viking silver hoard worth over $80,000 and well on his way to bigger and better things, taught David how to dowse for treasure with remarkable results. David suddenly found himself having to report a string of real treasures in the form of caches of Iron Age gold coins and items of Roman, Saxon and medieval gold and silver jewellery. No less than 11 of David's finds were recorded under the Treasure Act since 1998 and David also has to maintain a shelf full of trophies he is continuously winning at the Swale Search and Recovery Club.

Printed in Great Britain
by Amazon